Sous Vide

DELICIOUS RECIPES AND PRECISION TECHNIQUES THAT GUARANTEE SMOKY, FALL-OFF-THE-BONE BBQ EVERY TIME

GREG MRVICH

Ulysses Press

Published by
Ulysses Press
P.O. Box 3440
Berkeley, CA 94703
www.ulyssespress.com

ISBN: 978-1-61243-781-1
Library of Congress Catalog Number: 2018930777

Printed in Canada by Marquis Book Printing
10 9 8 7 6 5 4 3 2 1

Acquisitions editor: Casie Vogel
Managing editor: Claire Chun
Project editor: Claire Sielaff
Editor: Renee Rutledge
Proofreader: Shayna Keyles
Front cover design: Raquel Castro
Cover photos: front © Elena Veselova/shutterstock.com; back © Greg Mrvich
Interior design/layout: what!design @ whatweb.com
Interior photos: © Greg Mrvich except page 14 red kettle grill © stockphoto-graf/
    shutterstock.com, gas grill © Pro3DArt/shutterstock.com, offset smoker © Daniel
    Migukov/shutterstock.com

Distributed by Publishers Group West

IMPORTANT NOTE TO READERS: This book is independently authored and published and no sponsorship or endorsement of this book by, and no affiliation with, any trademarked brands or products mentioned or pictured within is claimed or suggested. All trademarks that appear in ingredient lists, photographs, and elsewhere in this book belong to their respective owners and are used here for informational purposes only. The author and publisher encourage readers to patronize the quality brands mentioned and pictured in this book.

This book is dedicated to my lovely wife Karen,
who has always supported me.

Contents

Author's Preface

It's no secret that I'm what you'd call a "foodie." I love eating different things, and it's more of an experience for me than simply sustenance.

Most of the TV and online entertainment I watch is food related. I discovered that everyday people like me are sharing their creations on YouTube. I watched plenty of folks cooking barbecue, but noticed that there weren't really many YouTube channels dedicated exclusively to outdoor cooking. The videos were more or less random.

In September of 2009, my sister and brother-in-law were coming over for dinner, and I was going to smoke a pork shoulder for pulled pork. For whatever reason, I handed my wife our little video

camera and said, "Would you film me?" She did, and to tell you the truth, I had no plans to ever shoot another video.

As the video gained views, something happened that I didn't expect. I started getting comments and questions. Before I knew it, I was even getting private messages from a guy in Japan asking for help on how to cook "American BBQ Ribs." I think that was the hook, and I decided to shoot another video. And another, and another… Before I knew it, I had an outdoor cooking channel. All it needed was a name. I literally came up with the name "Ballistic BBQ" just prior to starting one of my videos.

Around this same time, many of my new YouTube friends were also starting their own channels. It was really cool to watch what was going on. We were all helping one another out as we grew together. Before long, there were several dedicated outdoor cooking channels on YouTube. This was a special time for me, and I feel very fortunate to have been a part of it.

My channel has grown into one of the top outdoor cooking channels on YouTube, and it has brought me many opportunities that I am very grateful for. I have shot videos for companies, big and small, and I even took on the role of Grill Master for the 2017 CMT Award's official viewing party in Nashville, Tennessee. The biggest reward I have received from this journey, however, are the friendships that I've made, including with viewers, fellow creators, and some of the business owners I have worked with. YouTube is truly a community, and this is something I didn't realize at first.

Thank you for showing interest in my book!

Cheers,

Greg Mrvich

Ballistic BBQ

All About Sous Vide

Some of my happiest memories growing up in sunny San Diego involve simply being outdoors, whether it was running around the fields I used to play in with my neighborhood friends, or hiking and fishing while on vacation in the Sierras with my family. Every day as the sun went down, we would build a fire outside and toast hot dogs and marshmallows on sticks. Cooking with fire was fascinating to me.

At home, this fascination continued when watching my dad or grandpa cook on the grill. I learned techniques as I watched them turn steaks and flip burgers. The aromas of food being cooked this way inspired awe in my young mind. I wasn't just smelling good food; it was reliving my fondest memories of sitting around a fire toasting those hot dogs and marshmallows. To this day, the smell of food being cooked outdoors brings back those wonderful memories of the past. It actually lifts my spirits and gets the endorphins pumping.

As I grew older, I continued this family legacy, and I'd like to say that I've maybe taken it a few steps further. San Diego is a true melting pot of cultures. We are right on the Mexican border, so fresh and vibrant Baja-style influences on our food is huge. San Diego also has a thriving Asian population, with markets catering to immigrants from Southeast Asia, as well as China, Japan, and Korea. A stroll through any of these markets fills my head with so many ideas, and fusing these flavors together can create some pretty exciting dishes!

I created the Ballistic BBQ channel as a way to share my passion for outdoor cooking and diverse culinary influences with others on YouTube. And believe me, I had no idea after shooting my first video in September of 2009 where this simple hobby would take me.

So, inside of this book, I am going to take you on a little journey. It is basically primal cooking meets hi-tech. The funny (and cool) thing is, these techniques work very well together, and they bring yet another dimension to the outdoor cooking experience, allowing you to spend more time with the friends and family that you are cooking for. This, to me, is what cooking outdoors is all about.

WHAT IS SOUS VIDE?

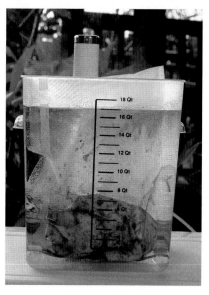

I'm going to kick this off with the hi-tech part. You see, sous vide actually does what we are trying to accomplish through barbecue. By using low temperatures to cook food for a long time, we break down connective tissues in tough cuts of meat, making them very tender and flavorful.

The one issue with traditional barbecue is that these techniques take time to master, and tough, dry meats are often the result for less experienced cooks.

Another aspect of traditional barbecue that may be a problem (for some) is the need to tend to and monitor the cooker. Falling asleep at the wrong time could result in losing your heat source all together, or having a bad spike in heat. Both of these situations could ruin your meal.

Sous vide (pronounced soo-veed) is a culinary technique which not too long ago was exclusive to professional chefs. It utilizes precise temperature control to deliver consistent results pretty much every time, which is why so many high-end restaurants have been using sous vide cooking for years to cook food to the exact level of doneness. Sous vide has recently become popular for home cooks due to the availability of affordable and easy-to-use sous vide precision-cooking equipment like the ones used in this book.

Sous vide literally means "under vacuum" in French. This is because the process involves vacuum-sealing food in a bag, then cooking it in a water bath, which is maintained at the desired temperature. The results of this precise temperature control with circulation produces results that are impossible to achieve through any other cooking method.

WHY SOUS VIDE?

Getting an expensive roast to the table cooked just the way you like it is critical. Doing this requires you to hit the meat's target temperature spot on; 5 or 10 degrees off can make a huge difference.

With traditional cooking methods like outdoor cooking, you don't have perfect control over heat and temperature. Consequently, it's very difficult and time consuming to consistently cook great food. Food can end up overcooked on the outside, with only a small portion in the center that is cooked to the temperature you want. You can end up with an expensive steak that is dried out, chewy, and flavorless.

When you are cooking meat in a hot environment, whether on a grill, a stovetop, or an oven, it will continue to cook even after it has been removed from the heat source. This is known as carryover cooking, one of the main culprits of ruining many a steak. Carryover cooking happens for two reasons: First, the exterior of the meat gets hot much more quickly than the interior. Second, because heat always moves from a hot to a cool area, so long as there is a difference in temperature between the outside of the meat and the inside, heat will keep moving from the surface to the center even after you remove the meat from the heat source. Carryover cooking will slow, and eventually stop, as internal and external temperatures approach each other and even out. But the process can result in a significant increase in temperature at the center of your steak, bringing it from a perfect pink to a disappointing gray.

With sous vide, you have precise temperature control. If you want your steak cooked medium rare, simply set the circulator to bring the water up to that temperature, which will be 130°F (54.4°C). Once the bagged steak is in the water bath, heat will still do what heat does...move from the hotter area to the cooler area and ultimately equalize. In other words, the entire steak will be 130°F. And since the environment it is cooking in is at 130°F, it will never go any higher.

Traditional cooking can require your constant attention. Sous vide cooking brings food to the exact temperature you want and holds it there. No need to worry about it overcooking.

IS SOUS VIDE SAFE?

Many people wonder if sous vide cooking is safe. University of California, Berkeley, addressed this in the July 2016 issue of *Berkeley Wellness*:

> A paper in the *International Journal of Gastronomy and Food Science* noted that if the [sous vided] food is consumed right away, there's no worry about the growth of pathogens... and there have been no reported outbreaks of foodborne illness from sous vide cooking.

In this book, the temperatures being referenced are the industry standards. You will notice that many are below the USDA standards for doneness. These are based on conventional cooking techniques, and there is a pasteurization effect that takes place during sous vide. This being said, feel free to adjust temperatures to fit your personal preference concerning doneness.

The simple takeaway is to use common sense while using this technique.

THE FINISHING PROCESS

Food, and in particular meat, is at the perfect temperature when it comes out of the sous vide bag it was cooked in. But it is missing something very important—a sear, or in the case of larger cuts like brisket, that smoky crust we all strive for when we're cooking outdoors. This is an added layer of flavor that will push whatever meat you cooked sous vide completely over the top!

When we finish off the cooking process on our sous vide foods, something magical happens: caramelization. This causes vegetables to develop a deeper, sweeter flavor. Meat becomes more savory, thanks to the Maillard reaction, where proteins are broken down into amino acids, which react with the carbohydrates that are present to produce the scent and wonderfully satisfying taste we crave. Smoke adds another layer of spicy or even sweet flavors, bringing the caveman/woman/person out of us!

Many people will finish their sous vide food off with a blow torch or in the broiler, and this does the job, but you're not going to get the same levels of flavor you'd get from finishing on a grill or in a smoker. This is why whenever I cook sous vide, I opt to finish the job outside.

All About Barbecue

In the US, throwing out the word barbecue (barbeque, BBQ, BBQUE) can get tempers flaring. Since getting involved in the community of outdoor cooks, I have had the opportunity to chat with people all around the world on what the word "barbecue" means to them. I've found it really depends on where they live, and what and how they like to cook outdoors. Ultimately, this is an argument that cannot be won. To many here in the US, barbecue has become somewhat of a blanket term describing anything that is cooked outdoors. To others, it has to be cooked at a low temperature for a long period of time to be considered barbecue. In some regions of our country, the type of protein defines barbecue. Like I said, this is an argument that has no winner, so I will define it this way: Smoking is barbecuing, and grilling is grilling.

GRILLING

A grill is a piece of outdoor cooking equipment where the cooking surface consists of an open rack or grate. The heat source underneath can be open flame, charcoal, gas, or electricity. The food is cooked directly on the rack or grate, taking advantage of the intense heat's searing effect. The best kinds of foods for cooking on a grill tend to be meats and poultry, but with proper technique, firm fish, seafood, and vegetables can be cooked on the grill as well.

One of the characteristics of food cooked on a grill are those sexy grill marks from the cooking grate or rack. Because a grill cooks at a high temperature with dry heat, its ability to sear is maximized, taking full advantage of the Maillard reaction. But, one also has to take care to keep meats from becoming overcooked and dried out.

The word "grill" can also be used as a verb to indicate cooking on a grill. And, of course, as discussed earlier, it can be used interchangeably with the word "barbecue." Most will agree, however, that barbecuing is a form of grilling over wood or charcoal.

SMOKING/BARBECUING

Smoking is what the majority of the outdoor cooking community will say is actually barbecuing. It is essentially cooking food using low heat for a long period of time. Barbecuing is often done with indirect heat. The heat source is connected to the chamber where the meat is held, or by arranging your charcoal away from the meat (two-zone cooking), if using a conventional grill. Unlike with grilling, the meat is not directly over the flames. Charcoal or wood are commonly used as the heat source for barbecue. Different types of wood give off different smoky flavors that the meat can absorb. In our early history, this technique originated to tenderize tougher cuts of meat like brisket, or preserve meats like ham and bacon, for long-term storage.

GRILLING AND SMOKING SETUPS

There are endless examples of cookers out there, so I'm just going to touch on the basics here. Pretty much any type of cooker available will work fine with the techniques and recipes contained in this book. Let's start with grills.

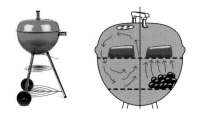

KETTLE GRILL: This is without a doubt the most popular charcoal grill in the US, if not the world, and no outdoor cook should be without one. This retro beauty is so versatile! You can grill over direct heat, or arrange the coals off to one side for indirect zone cooking, so you can go low 'n' slow.

GAS GRILL: The purist will turn their nose to this grill, but there is no disputing the fact that more people in the United States own a "gasser" than any other cooker. Even though this isn't cooking on an open flame, you can still draw great flavor from a gas grill. When you're cooking over direct heat, the juices drip onto deflectors, causing them to vaporize. The vapor rises and penetrates the food you are cooking. You can utilize the ability to shut down half of the burners for two-zone cooking. With a container of woodchips on the burner side and the food on the indirect heat side, guess what? You're smoking!

OFFSET SMOKER: This is probably one of the most common smokers in the United States. The heat source is contained in a fire box located at the side of the cooking chamber. Heat and smoke is drawn through the chamber and exits through the chimney stack. The temperature is controlled by opening and closing dampers located on the fire box and stack. Since the larger versions of this cooker are often fueled by small logs, they are referred to as "stick burners."

CERAMIC COOKER (KAMADO): Based on 3,000-year-old Chinese technology, the Kamado is one of the most versatile on the market and one of my all-time favorite cookers to use. Not only can you grill and smoke on it, but you can bake! The Kamado cooks with indirect heat when you use a deflector, which is a ceramic plate that forces the rising heat to flow around the sides and out the top damper. This is a very efficient form of convection cooking. To grill, you simply cook without the deflector, and you're rockin' intense direct heat.

CABINET SMOKER: These are terrific smokers and come in a variety of sizes. Essentially, they're an insulated cabinet with several racks, stacked vertically. The heat source (wood and charcoal) is located in a metal basket at the bottom of the cooker. Above the charcoal basket are a deflector and a water pan to maintain stable heat and humidity in the cooker. The heat is directed through channels so it enters the cooker through the top and exits through the stack opening at the bottom. This creates true convection in what is referred to as "reverse flow" in the outdoor cooking world. These are very efficient cookers that can cook a lot of food for such a small footprint.

Temperature Control

Like your stovetop, grills don't really have a temperature control, just a spectrum of low to high heat. To test the heat level of your grill, hover your hand over the direct heat and count the seconds before you can no longer tolerate the heat. Below is a rough guide of heat levels based on the length of time before you must move your hand away from the grill:

HIGH	1–3 seconds
MEDIUM-HIGH	4–5 seconds
MEDIUM	6–7 seconds
MEDIUM-LOW	8-10 seconds
LOW	11+ seconds

A smokers is more like an oven—it's a closed cooking vessel and temperatures are controlled by the dampers. Smoker controls vary greatly, however.

DRUM SMOKER: Drum cookers, like the Pit Barrel Cooker, are commercially available, but then there are the "ugly drum smokers," which are usually homemade. Though some of them really don't live up to the name "ugly"— there are some pretty cool drum cookers out there! In the community, the homemade version is referred to as a UDS.

They are very efficient and, like the cabinet smoker, take up a relatively small footprint. The charcoal and wood burn in a basket at the bottom of the drum. Dampers, at the bottom and top of the drum, control temperatures.

CHOOSING COOKING WOOD

This section identifies cooking woods for both grilling and smoking. I've listed some of the more popular woods, as well as some that have been recently making the scene.

MILD: Generally pretty mild, with hints of sweetness and fruitiness, fruit woods include apple, cherry, peach, and even citrus woods like orange and lemon. They pair well with the mild proteins like pork and poultry. Citrus woods have recently become popular with seafood.

MEDIUM: Big hitters in the smoking world, medium woods are terrific for most proteins, with the exception of maybe fish (for fish, I'd definitely stay in the mild category). Oak and most of the nut woods, such as hickory, almond, and pecan, fall in this category. They all have a slight sweetness, but produce a spicier flavor than fruit woods do. Use on beef, pork, chicken, and lamb.

HEAVY: Without a doubt, mesquite is the heaviest cooking wood out there. Be very careful when smoking with this wood, as it can overpower the food. It is wonderful for grilling, though. Allow the wood chunks to burn down and you have the perfect platform for steaks. I also count walnut as a heavy wood. It works well when mixed with lighter woods. Heavy woods are best used with beef.

CHARCOAL CHOICES

There are basically two types of charcoal to choose from: briquettes and lump charcoal.

Briquettes are the very familiar square, pillow-shaped variety that many of us grew up with. They are a combination of charcoal and other ingredients molded into easy-to-light lumps. Kingsford, the most popular brand in the US, uses bits of charcoal, coal, starch (as a binder), sawdust, and sodium nitrate (to make it burn better). This same brand has recently created a line of 100% natural briquettes in response to the negative opinions on binders and nitrates. Briquettes burn very consistently, both temperature-wise and with their burn time. Because of this, they are an excellent choice when baking outdoors or using certain types of cookers.

Lump charcoal can be made from a variety of hardwoods. The most popular are oak and mesquite. The manufacturers basically cook the wood in kilns until it turns into carbon. The benefits of lump

are the great smoky flavor it adds to food, the high temperatures it can obtain, and with no binders, the very clean burn. The ash left by lump is much lighter than the ash left by briquettes. Some of the negatives with lump are the inconsistencies with burn time and temperatures, plus much of the charcoal toward the bottom of the bag consists of unusable crumbs and the occasional rocks. Negatives aside, it is my go-to when it comes to charcoal.

There are three ways to light your charcoal: 1. lighter fluid (don't you dare!), 2. chimney starter, and 3. propane torch.

Lighter fluid works but the problem is flavor—it can leave behind the taste of kerosene, which will ruin any meal. NEVER use lighter fluid in a ceramic cooker. The gas flavors will penetrate the porous ceramic and come to life every time you cook on it. NOT GOOD!

A chimney starter is a wonderful choice for any type of charcoal. Usually, a small amount of wadded-up newspaper is placed under the chimney, which is loaded with charcoal. The paper is lit on fire, which subsequently ignites the charcoal.

My personal favorite is a propane torch, with which you can prearrange your charcoal while it is unlit. Then, simply point the torch at the charcoal and blast away! This is particularly good when using a technique such as a Snake Burn, also known as the Minion Method.

The Minion Method

A competitive pit master named Jim Minion gets to claim inventing this technique. Simply put, pile lit charcoal on top of prearranged, unlit charcoal. The lit charcoal starts a chain reaction of slowly igniting the unlit charcoal, which gives the outdoor cook a longer burn time for smoking. By arranging the charcoal in a line around the inner wall of a kettle grill, you are able to turn this humble cooker into a very effecting smoker.

SAUCES AND GLAZES

Many think that sauce is what defines barbecue. Well, it's not. Remember, it is how the food is cooked that makes it barbecue.

Others will say that sauce makes the meat tastier, enhancing the flavors that the cooking process introduced. Still others will argue that sauce ruins those flavors. Like I said before, there is no winning these barbecue arguments. The best course to follow is to cook food the way you and your loved ones like it.

If you like sauce (like I do), then here are some basic recipes from different regions around the US. Feel free to modify any of these recipes!

CAROLINA MUSTARD-BASED BBQ SAUCE

This is a sweet and tangy sauce.

1 cup yellow mustard

¼ cup packed light brown sugar

¼ cup honey

2 tablespoons Worcestershire sauce

¼ cup apple cider vinegar

½ teaspoon coarse-ground kosher or sea salt

½ teaspoon freshly ground black pepper

1 teaspoon Louisiana hot sauce

1 tablespoon butter

Whisk together all of the ingredients, with the exception of the butter, in a medium saucepan. Bring to a boil over medium heat, reduce heat, and whisk in the tablespoon of butter. Allow at least 30 minutes to cool before using.

KANSAS CITY BBQ SAUCE

This is the classic barbecue sauce that most people think of. Sweet, with just a bit of heat and acidity.

1 cup ketchup

1 (6-ounce) can tomato paste

1 cup light brown sugar

½ cup apple cider vinegar

3 tablespoons dark molasses

½ teaspoon coarse-ground kosher or sea salt

½ teaspoon garlic powder

½ teaspoon celery seed

½ teaspoon freshly ground black pepper

½ teaspoon cayenne pepper

½ teaspoon ground cinnamon

1 tablespoon butter

Whisk together all of the ingredients, with the exception of the butter, in a medium saucepan. Bring to a boil over medium heat, then reduce heat and simmer, uncovered, until thickened. Whisk in the butter, then remove from heat, allowing to cool at least 30 minutes before use.

EASTERN CAROLINA VINEGAR SAUCE

If you're used to Kansas City–style BBQ sauce, then hold on to your hat! Eastern Carolina sauce is all about the vinegar and crushed red pepper. There is no arguing this!

3 cups apple cider vinegar

1 cup light brown sugar

2 teaspoons crushed red pepper

2 teaspoons coarse-ground kosher or sea salt

1 teaspoon freshly ground black pepper

1 teaspoon cayenne pepper

Whisk together all of the ingredients in a medium saucepan, bringing it to a boil over medium–high heat. Stir mixture until sugar melts completely, then allow 30 minutes to cool.

BOURBON BBQ GLAZE

My personal favorite, this is basically a little twist on Kansas City BBQ Sauce that's pumped up with some spicy, oaky bourbon.

1 cup ketchup

1 (6-ounce) can tomato paste

1 cup dark brown sugar

½ cup apple cider vinegar

½ cup bourbon

3 tablespoons dark molasses

½ teaspoon fresh ground kosher or sea salt

½ teaspoon garlic powder

½ teaspoon celery seed

½ teaspoon freshly ground black pepper

½ teaspoon cayenne pepper

½ teaspoon pickling spice

1 tablespoon butter

Whisk together all of the ingredients, with the exception of the butter, in a medium saucepan. Bring to a boil over medium heat, then reduce heat and simmer, uncovered, for about 1 hour. You want to both thicken the sauce and soften the pickling spice. Whisk in the butter, then remove from heat, allowing to cool at least 30 minutes before use.

RUBS AND SEASONING

Here are two all–purpose (AP) barbecue rubs. Rubs pretty much all have the same basic base ingredients. Play around with additional spices to make these recipes your own!

AP RUB #1

YIELD: about ¾ cup

¼ cup packed light brown sugar

2 tablespoons fresh ground kosher or sea salt

2 tablespoons garlic powder

2 tablespoons freshly ground black pepper

2 tablespoons smoked paprika

2 teaspoons onion powder

1 teaspoon ground coriander

1 teaspoon ground cinnamon

½ teaspoon ground cumin

Mix all of the ingredients together in a small bowl. Store in an airtight container in a cool, dark place for up to 1 month.

AP RUB #2

YIELD: about 1 cup

⅓ cup packed dark brown sugar

1 tablespoon raw sugar

¼ cup smoked paprika

3 tablespoons coarse-ground kosher or sea salt

2 teaspoons onion powder

2 teaspoons garlic powder

2 teaspoons celery seed

1 teaspoon cayenne pepper

1 teaspoon allspice

Mix all of the ingredients together in a small bowl. Store in an airtight container in a cool, dark place for up to 1 month.

BEEF SEASONING

YIELD: about ½ cup

2 tablespoons black peppercorns

1 tablespoon whole mustard seeds

2 teaspoons dill seeds

1 teaspoon coriander seeds

4 teaspoons coarse-ground kosher or sea salt

4 teaspoons dried minced garlic

1 tablespoon dried onion flakes

1 teaspoon crushed red pepper flakes

1 teaspoon paprika

Cook peppercorns, mustard seeds, dill seeds, and coriander seeds in a small skillet over medium heat, stirring until the seeds begin to pop and become fragrant, about 2 minutes. Transfer to a mortar and pestle and coarsely crush, or place in a sturdy plastic bag and crush with a heavy skillet or meat hammer. Add the salt, garlic, onion flakes, red pepper flakes, and paprika. Crush to combine ingredients.

Sous Vide Gear

There are tons of gadgets out there marketed for sous vide. Some are useful and some, not so much. This section is a quick overview of what you'll need to get started with sous vide based on my knowledge of equipment that I have and use.

CIRCULATORS

The most important component of sous vide, the circulator brings up the water bath temperature and, more importantly, maintains the target temperature you selected. Nowadays, the home cook can choose from several circulators, with prices ranging from under $100 and up. I'm going to provide you with the pros and cons of the circulators I own.

JOULE BY CHEFSTEPS: This is probably my favorite circulator. The sleek-looking unit is user friendly and runs through an app from your wireless device via WiFi or Bluetooth. The app is fun and even has recipes for you to try out. If you're not sure of the target temperature, you can cook your meat in cross sections and simply select what you want the finished product to look like. Of course, you can also punch in your target temperature. The only con is the fact that it can only be programmed through the app. There are no manual controls to get Joule up and running, which means that if you cannot connect to the unit with your device, the circulator is useless.

ANOVA SOUS VIDE PRECISION COOKER WITH BLUETOOTH: A great buy, this Anova model is effective, very simple to operate, and comes with a handy app for your wireless device. This particular circulator can only be controlled via Bluetooth, but Anova does make a unit that has a WiFi feature. The app is user friendly, and has recipes and tutorial videos. The one feature that I love is the ability to manually control the temperature settings simply by manipulating a dial on the front of the unit.

VACMASTER SV1 SOUS VIDE COOKING IMMERSION CIRCULATOR: This is the circulator that got me into sous vide. It was actually given to me by a good friend and awesome cook (thanks, John!). With 1500 watts of power, the SV1 is really geared toward commercial use. Flip on the power and dial the temperature up or down using arrow buttons. A timer feature uses up/down buttons as well. This straightforward circulator is a workhorse and really does the job. The only drawbacks are its size compared to my other circulators and the fact that it does not have a wireless feature.

TRAVELLOR SOUS VIDE IMMERSION CIRCULATOR: A pretty inexpensive unit only available online, this circulator has no real frills, such as the ability to connect to a device or an app. I have checked the water temperatures using a very accurate thermometer and it seems to be spot-on. My one complaint is it's just not as easy to set as my other circulators. Sometimes I find myself fumbling around with the controls and it will not circulate until you set its timer.

Circulators from left to right: Joule, Anova, VacMaster SV1, and TRAVELLOR.

OPTIONAL EQUIPMENT

SOUS VIDE BALLS: I highly recommend these! With very long cooks (like 48 hours), evaporation is a concern. You can control this by covering your bath with foil or a lid, or simply tossing in a bunch of these balls. Pretty much like smaller ping pong balls, but made out of a heavier plastic, these will also help the circulator bring the water temperature up more quickly. (Many chefs use ping pong balls, by the way.) Some brands to look at are PolyScience and Sammic.

SOUS VIDE TUB: You can use any type of container you wish for sous vide. Many people simply use pots, but I like using large clear containers. The nice thing is you can buy sizes perfect for cooking large cuts of meat, like ribs or briskets. Plus, you can see what's going on inside of the bath. This is important when it comes to issues such as a leaky bag. EVERIE, Cambro, and Rubbermaid are brands I like.

BATH LID: A nice thing about using sous vide tubs are the lids. They fit like a glove, but the cutouts available are limited. Lids are normally sold separately.

RIB RACK: You can find cool expandable rib racks online for a decent price. I'll tell you the truth, however, the only time I ever use one is to weight down "floaters," or foods that float, such as corn, apples and artichokes. Note: you can also just throw a few butter knives in a bag and it will do just fine as a weight.

VACUUM SEALER: As discussed earlier, sous vide literally means "under vacuum" in French. This is because, traditionally, the food to be cooked is vacuum sealed by being immersed in the water bath. Vacuum sealers have become very affordable to the home consumer recently. Plus, they come in handy for daily use like preserving leftovers and such. I use a basic FoodSaver vacuum sealer, which does the job just fine. If you don't have a vacuum sealer, you can use the immersion technique to seal your bags (see Immersion Technique sidebar below).

SOUS VIDE CLAMPS: Another accessory you may consider buying, especially if you will not be using a vacuum sealer, are sous vide clamps. These keep the bags from drifting around in the bath by clamping the tops of the bags to the rim of the tub. They would come in handy if using the immersion technique (see below) instead of vacuum sealing.

Immersion Technique

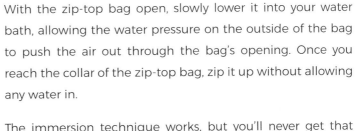

What is the immersion technique? It is simply placing the food to be cooked sous vide in a zip-top bag instead of using a vacuum sealer. Here's how you do it.

With the zip-top bag open, slowly lower it into your water bath, allowing the water pressure on the outside of the bag to push the air out through the bag's opening. Once you reach the collar of the zip-top bag, zip it up without allowing any water in.

The immersion technique works, but you'll never get that perfect airtight environment like you do with a vacuum-seal bag. Plus, when cooking veggies in a vacuum-seal bag, you can toss them in the freezer as is, without the risk of freezer burn.

Beef

COFFEE-RUBBED PORTERHOUSE STEAK

This steak recipe pairs a nice earthy savoriness with just the right bite of pepper.

PREP TIME: 20 minutes   **COOK TIME:** 2 hours sous vide, plus 2–4 minutes on grill   **SERVES:** 1–2

1 (8- to 16-ounce) porterhouse steak
¼ cup coarse-ground kosher or sea salt
¼ cup freshly ground black pepper

2 tablespoons ground coffee
1 tablespoon raw sugar
1 tablespoon vegetable oil

1. Preheat a water bath by setting the sous vide circulator to 130°F (54.4°C).

2. Place steak, unseasoned, in vacuum-seal bag or medium zip-top bag.

3. Place the bag in the water bath (use the immersion technique on page 23 if you are using a zip-top bag), and the set timer for 2 hours.

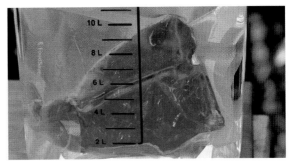

4. To make the rub, thoroughly mix the salt, pepper, ground coffee, and raw sugar in a small bowl.

FINISHING STEPS

5. About 20 minutes before the 2-hour sous vide period ends, light charcoal for direct cooking, or preheat a gas grill.

6. After the timer goes off, remove the bag from the water bath. Remove the steak from the bag and blot with a dry paper towel.

7. Brush on the vegetable oil, then generously season the steak with the coffee rub.

8. Place the steak on a hot grill for about 1 minute per side, until well browned and crusted.

9. Transfer the steak to a cutting board and let rest for 5 minutes. Serve.

ALL-AMERICAN CHEESEBURGER

Nothing screams America like a good old-fashioned cheeseburger! You can keep this tradition and say goodbye to dry patties, thanks to sous vide.

PREP TIME: 50 minutes   **COOK TIME:** 20 minutes sous vide, plus 1–2 minutes on grill   **SERVES:** 2

1 pound 80% lean/20% fat ground beef

2 slices American cheese

2 sesame buns

coarse-ground kosher or sea salt, to taste

TOPPINGS:

lettuce

onions, sliced

dill pickles, sliced

tomatoes, sliced

mayo

mustard

ketchup

1. On top of a sheet of parchment paper, divide the beef into two sections. Form your first beef patty by rolling the first section into a ball then flattening it to a diameter slightly larger than the buns to compensate for shrinkage. I like to use a ring form to get that perfect shape.

2. Once your patties are done, use a knife to cut a square of parchment around each patty. This makes them easy to pick up.

3. Place the patties in the freezer for 20–30 minutes until they become firm enough so that the vacuum-seal bag does not squish them. You do not want them to freeze solid.

4. While the patties firm up, preheat a water bath by setting the sous vide circulator to 135°F (57.2°C).

5. Once the patties are no longer soft, place them in a bag and vacuum seal. You can also use a zip-top bag.

6. Place bag in the water bath (use the immersion technique on page 23 if you are using a zip-top bag), and set the timer for 20 minutes. Light charcoal for direct cooking, or preheat a gas grill.

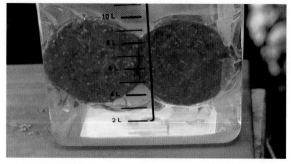

7. After the timer goes off, remove the bag from the water bath. Remove the patties from the bag and blot with a dry paper towel. Season with salt.

FINISHING STEPS

8. Grill patties over direct heat for about 30 seconds per side. Toast buns (if desired) on indirect side of the grill.

9. Immediately after first flip, place cheese on patties.

10. Assemble burger with desired toppings and condiments.

11. Enjoy!

SANTA MARIA TRI-TIP

Tri-tip is a beautifully tender and flavorful cut of meat from the bottom sirloin of a steer. Its roots are in Santa Maria, California, and it is the primary cut used in Santa Maria–style barbecue.

PREP TIME: 20 minutes   **COOK TIME:** 6 hours sous vide, plus 5 minutes on grill   **SERVES:** 4–6

1 (2–3 pound) tri-tip roast
4 cloves garlic, crushed
1–2 tablespoons olive oil

coarse-ground kosher or sea salt, to taste
freshly ground black pepper, to taste
1 tablespoon vegetable oil

1. Preheat a water bath by setting the sous vide circulator to 130°F (54.4°C).

2. Trim any silver skin or excess fat from the roast.

3. Spread crushed garlic on each side of the roast, then place in a medium zip-top bag or vacuum-seal bag with the crushed garlic on each side. Drizzle with the olive oil, then seal.

4. Place the tri-tip in the water bath (use the immersion technique on page 23 if you are using a zip-top bag), and set the timer for 6 hours.

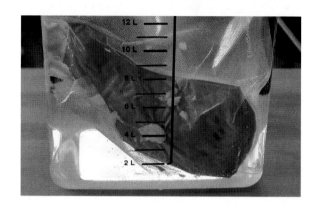

FINISHING STEPS

5. Twenty minutes before the timer goes off, light charcoal for direct cooking, or preheat a gas grill.

6. After the timer has gone off, remove the tri-tip from the bag and blot with a dry paper towel.

7. Brush a small amount of vegetable oil to both sides of the roast and season liberally with salt and pepper.

8. Grill on all sides over direct heat until a nice crust appears, 1–2 minutes each side.

9. Remove from the grill and let rest for 15 minutes.

10. Slice the tri-tip against the grain and serve.

KOREAN GRILLED BEEF SHORT RIBS

Savory, sweet, tender, sticky ribs! There are so many layers of flavors in this recipe, your taste buds are going to spring into overdrive.

This is a pretty traditional Korean recipe, but the sous vide twist takes the tenderness to another level.

PREP TIME: 30 minutes, plus 4 hours to marinate minutes on grill **SERVES:** 3–4   **COOK TIME:** 4 hours sous vide, plus 2–5

1 Asian pear (or any sweet, firm variety), peeled, cored, and chopped

½ cup water

6 cloves garlic

3 green onions, chopped, divided

1 tablespoon toasted sesame oil

½ cup mirin (rice wine)

¼ cup white wine vinegar

1 cup soy sauce

2–2½ pounds beef short ribs cut flanken style (across the bone)

1. Preheat a water bath by setting the sous vide circulator to 135° F (59° C).

2. Combine Asian pear, water, garlic, 2 chopped green onions, sesame oil, mirin, white wine vinegar, and soy sauce in a food processor or blender and process well to create a marinade.

3. Place the ribs in a zip-top bag and pour in marinade, assuring all pieces of meat are coated. Marinate in refrigerator a minimum of 4 hours and no longer than 24 hours.

4. After marinating period is complete, remove ribs from the bag and allow excess marinade to drain off naturally over a bowl or sink.

5. Place the ribs in a vacuum-seal bag or a fresh zip-top bag.

6. Place the ribs in the water bath (use the immersion technique on page 23 if you are using a zip-top bag), and set the timer for 3 hours.

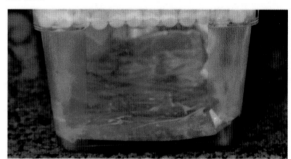

FINISHING STEPS

7. Twenty minutes before the timer goes off, light charcoal for direct cooking, or preheat a gas grill.

8. Remove the ribs from the bag and then blot dry with a paper towel.

9. Grill ribs over direct heat for about 30 seconds per side.

10. Garnish with the remaining chopped green onion.

BARBECUE BEEF BRISKET

Brisket is considered the king of meats when it comes to barbecue. It can take years to master this delicious cut, due to its tough texture. To do it right, the Pitmaster needs to go low and slow for hours to break it down. Cooking brisket sous vide takes away a lot of the guess work, sleep deprivation (from tending the smoker), and stress of dealing with the spikes and drops in your cooker's temperature.

PREP TIME: 45 minutes **COOK TIME:** 24 hours sous vide, plus 3 hours in smoker **SERVES:** 6-10

5- to 8-pound brisket flat
8 cloves garlic, crushed

1–2 tablespoons olive oil
½ cup Beef Seasoning (page 20)

1. Preheat a water bath by setting the sous vide circulator to 155°F (68.3°C).

2. Trim off the excess silver skin and fat cap down to about ¼-inch thick.

3. Place the brisket in a zip-top or vacuum-seal bag with the garlic and the olive oil drizzled on both sides.

4. Place the brisket in the water bath (use the immersion technique on page 23 if you are using a zip-top bag), and set the timer for 24 hours.

FINISHING STEPS

5. Preheat your smoker to 250°F (121.1°C), adding the wood of your choice, about 45 minutes to 1 hour prior to removing the meat from the sous vide bath.

6. Remove the brisket from the bag and blot with a dry paper towel.

7. Generously season both sides of brisket with the Beef Seasoning (you can also substitute this with ¼ cup coarse-ground salt and ¼ cup freshly ground black pepper).

8. Place the brisket in the smoker. Set the timer for 3 hours.

9. Remove the brisket from the smoker and rest for about 30 minutes.

10. Slice the rested brisket across the grain in ¼-thick slices and serve.

STANDING PRIME RIB ROAST

This beautiful beef roast is a favorite on the holidays, and for good reason. So tender, flavorful, and juicy—it is a crowd-pleaser! It is also pretty expensive and can be tricky to cook just right.

Fear no more. Sous vide is here to save the day! When selecting a prime rib, count on two people fed for each bone on the roast. Request that your butcher separate the bones, then truss them back on with twine.

PREP TIME: 30 minutes **COOK TIME:** 6 hours sous vide, plus 5 minutes on grill **SERVES:** 4-6

5- to 6-pound rib roast
2–3 tablespoons olive oil
5 cloves garlic, crushed
2–3 sprigs fresh rosemary

6–8 sprigs fresh thyme
2 tablespoons vegetable oil, for brushing
coarse-ground kosher or sea salt, to taste
freshly ground black pepper, to taste

1. Preheat a water bath by setting the sous vide circulator to 135°F (57.2°C).

2. Place the roast in a vacuum-seal or zip-top bag with the olive oil, crushed garlic, and fresh herbs on the top and bottom of roast.

3. Place the roast in the water bath (use the immersion technique on page 23 if you are using a zip-top bag), and set the timer for 6 hours.

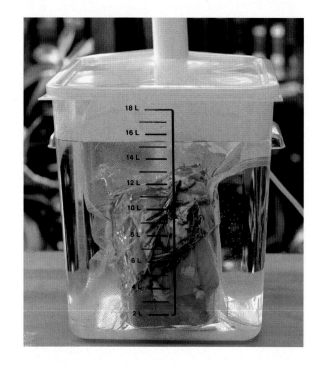

FINISHING STEPS

4. Preheat grill for direct heat 20 minutes prior to removing the roast from the sous vide bath.

5. Remove the roast from the bag and blot with a dry paper towel.

6. Apply a little vegetable oil to all sides of the roast and season generously with the salt and pepper.

7. Grill the roast on all sides over direct heat until a nice crust develops, about 5 minutes.

8. Remove from the grill and allow 20–30 minutes for roast to rest.

9. Remove butcher twine and separate ribs, then slice roast in ½- to 1-inch slices and serve.

BEEF SHORT RIBS

Sweet, tender meat adorns these (often huge) bones. In the outdoor cooking world, this cut is lovingly referred to as "Dino Bones." The nickname pays homage to a certain caveman cartoon from the good old days.

This recipe will produce braised tender ribs that will blow your friends and family away!

PREP TIME: 30 minutes   **COOK TIME:** 12 hours sous vide, plus 3 hours on grill or smoker
SERVES: 2–4

4 bone rack of beef short ribs

barbecue sauce of your choice

1. Preheat a water bath by setting the sous vide circulator to 185°F (85°C).

2. With a sharp knife, score and remove the membrane from the backside of the ribs.

3. Remove any excess fat and silver skin from the meat side of the ribs.

4. Place rack of ribs in a vacuum-seal or zip-top bag.

5. Place ribs in water bath (use the immersion technique on page 23 if you are using a zip-top bag), and set the timer for 12 hours.

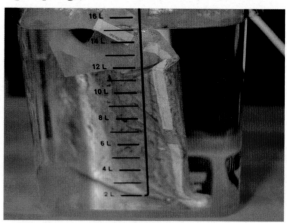

FINISHING STEPS

6. Twenty minutes prior to removing the ribs from the sous vide bath, preheat the grill (I used my kettle grill) to 250°F (121.1°C) for indirect heat.

7. Remove the ribs from the bag, blot with a dry paper towel, and slice between each bone, separating the ribs from each other.

8. Place the ribs on a cookie rack and brush on a light coating of barbecue sauce.

9. Place on the smoker and smoke for 3 hours.

10. Remove from the cooker, allow 10–15 minutes to rest, then serve.

CARNE ASADA TACOS

You're going to love this authentic recipe for one of the most popular street foods in Mexico. Why sous vide? The sous vide process not only makes the thin cut of inexpensive beef as tender as filet mignon, but it also lets the flavor of the marinade penetrate like no other technique.

PREP TIME: 30 minutes, plus 8–12 hours to marinate   **COOK TIME:** 6 hours sous vide, plus 2–4 minutes on grill   **SERVES:** 8–12

¼ cup fresh lime juice

4 cloves garlic

1 white onion, chopped

½ cup fresh orange juice

½ cup chopped green onion, plus more to garnish

1 tablespoon coarse-ground kosher or sea salt, plus more to taste

¼ cup olive oil

1–2 jalapeno peppers, minced

2 tablespoons distilled white vinegar

1 tablespoon dried Mexican oregano

½ cup dark Mexican beer

3 pounds beef flap or flank steak

freshly ground black pepper, to taste

corn tortillas, to serve

chopped fresh cilantro, to garnish

Cotija cheese, to garnish

salsa, to garnish

fresh limes, to serve

1. Place the lime juice, garlic, white onion, orange juice, green onion, salt, olive oil, peppers, white vinegar, oregano, and beer in a medium glass bowl, and mix well with a wooden spoon.

2. Place meat in a plastic zip-top bag, and pour the marinade over the meat. Massage the outside of the bag with your hands to assure that all of the surface area of the meat is covered in the marinade. Close the zip-top bag and place it in the refrigerator for 8–12 hours.

3. Preheat a water bath by setting the sous vide circulator to 135°F (57.2°C).

4. After the marinating period has ended, remove the meat from the bag. Hold the meat over your sink and allow excess liquid to fall naturally from the meat. You want it to have some marinade on it during the sous vide process.

5. Place the meat in a vacuum-seal bag or zip-top bag.

6. Immerse the meat in the water bath (use the immersion technique on page 23 if you are using a zip-top bag), and set the timer for 6 hours.

FINISHING STEPS

7. About 20 minutes prior to removing the meat from the sous vide bath, light charcoal for direct cooking, or preheat a gas grill.

8. Remove the meat from the bag, blot it with a dry paper towel, and season with salt and black pepper.

9. Grill the meat over hot direct heat for about 1 minute per side, until nice char marks form.

10. After meat is removed from the grill, heat up the corn tortillas.

11. Let the meat rest about 5 minutes, then slice the meat across the grain, into bite-size pieces.

12. Add meat to tortilla and garnish with chopped cilantro and fresh green onion, topping with Cotija cheese, salsa, and a squeeze of fresh lime.

GRILLED RIBEYE STEAK

Tender, juicy, and oh so flavorful is the best way to describe this fatty cut of goodness from the rib area of the steer. An all-time favorite, and a perfect match for both sous vide and the grill!

PREP TIME: 20 minutes   **COOK TIME:** 2 hours sous vide, plus 2–4 minutes on grill   **SERVES:** 1–2 per steak

1 (8- to 16-ounce) ribeye steak
1 pat unsalted butter

coarse-ground kosher or sea salt, to taste
freshly ground black pepper, to taste

1. Preheat a water bath by setting the sous vide circulator to 130°F (54.4°C).

2. Place the steak in a vacuum-seal bag or zip-top bag with one pat of butter on each side of the steak.

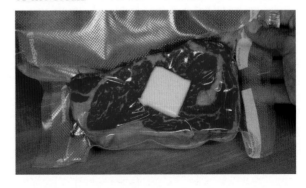

3. Immerse the steak in the water bath (use the immersion technique on page 23 if you are using a zip-top bag), and set the timer for 2 hours.

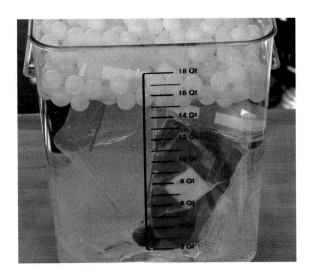

FINISHING STEPS

4. About 20 minutes prior to removing the steak from the water bath, light charcoal for direct cooking, or preheat a gas grill.

5. Remove the steak from the bag and blot with a dry paper towel.

6. Season both sides of the steak with salt and pepper.

7. Grill the steak over direct heat for 1–2 minutes on each side, assuring that the edges get grilled as well.

8. Allow the steak to rest for 5 minutes, slice, then serve.

BEEF TENDERLOIN (FILET MIGNON)

Tenderloin is beef royalty! Order this cut in a chop house and you'll be shelling out some big bucks. You'll save a lot of cash cooking it at home, but it's still not a budget meal, especially if you buy prime. Sous vide will allow you to easily cook this melt-in-your-mouth cut of beef to perfection!

PREP TIME: 15 minutes   **COOK TIME:** 2 hours sous vide, plus 2–4 minutes on the grill   **SERVES:** 2

2 (6- to 10-ounce) tenderloin fillets
4 cloves garlic, crushed
8 sprigs fresh thyme

2 tablespoons extra-virgin olive oil
coarse-ground kosher or sea salt
freshly ground black pepper

1. Preheat a water bath by setting the sous vide circulator to 130°F (54.4°C).

2. Tie butcher's twine around each fillet, forming them into a circular shape. Trim excess twine with a knife.

3. Place the fillets in a vacuum-seal bag or zip-top bag with the crushed garlic, thyme, and olive oil on both sides.

4. Immerse the sealed fillets in the water bath (use the immersion technique on page 23 if you are using a zip-top bag), and set the timer for 2 hours.

FINISHING STEPS

5. About 20 minutes before removing the meat from the sous vide bath, light charcoal for direct cooking, or preheat a gas grill.

6. Remove the fillets from the bag and blot with a dry paper towel.

7. Season fillets with salt and pepper.

8. Grill the fillets over direct heat, assuring that both sides and edges get browned.

9. Allow 4 minutes to rest, then serve.

SIRLOIN STEAK SANDWICH

Sirloin is a very inexpensive cut of meat with a delicious beefy flavor. However, it is fairly lean, so it can be a little on the tough side. Sous vide cooking will break down the tough connective tissue and make the humble sirloin steak as tender as filet mignon!

PREP TIME: 20 minutes   **COOK TIME:** 2 hours sous vide, plus 2–4 minutes on grill   **SERVES:** 2–4

2 (8- to 10-ounce) sirloin steaks

4 teaspoons olive oil, divided

4–6 sprigs fresh thyme

coarse-ground kosher or sea salt, to taste

freshly ground black pepper, to taste

2–4 buns or 4–8 slices sandwich bread, to serve

TOPPINGS:

mayo

lettuce

sliced tomato

1. Preheat a water bath by setting the sous vide circulator to 130°F (54.4°C).

2. Coat the steaks with 1 teaspoon of the olive oil each and place in a vacuum-seal bag or zip-top bag, along with the fresh thyme.

3. Immerse the steak in the water bath (use the immersion technique on page 23 if you are using a zip-top bag), and set the timer for 2 hours.

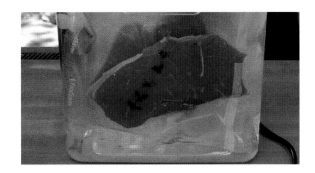

FINISHING STEPS

4. About 20 minutes prior to removing the meat from the sous vide bath, light charcoal for direct cooking, or preheat a gas grill.

5. Remove the steaks from the bag and blot with a dry paper towel.

6. Brush them with the remaining olive oil, then season both sides of the steak with salt and pepper.

7. Grill the steaks over direct heat for 1–2 minutes on each side.

8. Allow the steaks to rest for 5 minutes, then slice into ¼-inch-thick slices.

9. Dress the bun (or bread) with mayo, lettuce, and fresh sliced tomato, and top with sliced steak.

10. Enjoy!

GRILLED LONDON BROIL

London broil (for some reason) has been turned into a cut of meat, rather than what it really is—a method of preparing top round steak. Oh...and guess what? It has nothing to do with London. This is an American dish!

PREP TIME: 25 minutes, plus 4–8 hours to marinate   **COOK TIME:** 6–8 hours sous vide, plus 2–4 minutes on grill   **SERVES:** 5–6

1 cup soy sauce
1 tablespoon balsamic vinegar
3 cloves garlic, minced
1½ tablespoons olive oil
1 teaspoon chopped fresh rosemary
1 teaspoon chopped fresh thyme

½ teaspoon chopped fresh sage
1 teaspoon paprika
1 teaspoon freshly ground black pepper
coarse-ground kosher or sea salt, to taste
1½- to 2-pound top round steak

1. Mix all of the ingredients except the steak together in a bowl.

2. Place the meat in a plastic bag or bowl, and cover with the marinade. Refrigerate for 4–8 hours.

3. Preheat a water bath by setting the sous vide circulator to 130°F (54.4°C).

FINISHING STEPS

6. About 20 minutes prior to removing the steak from the sous vide bath, light charcoal for direct cooking, or preheat a gas grill.

7. Remove the steak from the bag and blot with a dry paper towel.

8. Season both sides of the steak with salt and pepper.

4. Place the steak in a vacuum-seal bag or zip-top bag with about 3 tablespoons of the marinade.

5. Immerse the steak in the water bath (use the immersion technique on page 23 if you are using a zip-top bag), and set the timer for 6–8 hours.

9. Grill the steak over direct heat for 1–2 minutes on each side.

10. Allow the steak to rest for 5 minutes, slice against the grain, then serve.

GRILLED VEAL CHOPS

Veal chops, one of the most expensive cuts of meat, can be very tender and subtle of flavor when cooked properly, but the margin for error is pretty narrow. This recipe is about as simple as simple can be. This cut is actually better when cooked more toward medium.

PREP TIME: 10 minutes **COOK TIME:** 3 hours sous vide, plus 4 minutes on grill **SERVES:** 2-4

1 bone-in veal chop per person
1 tablespoon olive oil

coarse-ground kosher or sea salt, to taste
freshly ground black pepper, to taste

1. Preheat a water bath by setting the sous vide circulator to 134°F (56.7°C).

2. Place the veal chops in vacuum-seal bags or zip-top bags.

3. Immerse the veal in the water bath (use the immersion technique on page 23 if you are using a zip-top bag), and set the timer for 3 hours.

FINISHING STEPS

4. Twenty minutes before the timer goes off, light charcoal for direct cooking, or preheat a gas grill.

5. Remove the veal chops from the bag and blot with a dry paper towel. Brush on a light coating of olive oil and season with the salt and pepper.

6. Grill the chops over direct heat for 1–2 minutes per side. If the chops are thick, make sure you get the edges as well!

7. Remove the chops from the cooker and allow 5–10 minutes to rest before serving.

Pork

PORK LOIN ROAST WITH APPLES AND ROSEMARY

Pork loin is very flavorful, but one of the leanest cuts of pork. Due to its lack of fat, everything needs to be on point, or you will end up with a dry, chewy mess! No more, thanks to sous vide!

PREP TIME: 30 minutes   **COOK TIME:** 6 hours sous vide, plus 5–10 minutes on grill   **SERVES:** 4–8

2 tablespoons chopped fresh rosemary

4 tablespoons brown sugar, divided

1 teaspoon freshly ground black pepper

1¼ teaspoons coarse-ground kosher or sea salt, divided

1 tablespoon olive oil

1 (4- to 6-pound) boneless pork loin roast

4 Granny Smith apples, peeled and sliced

juice from ½ lemon

3 tablespoons unsalted butter

2 sticks cinnamon bark (or 1 tablespoon ground)

¼ teaspoon ground nutmeg

⅛ teaspoon (or one whole split bean) vanilla extract

1 tablespoon vegetable oil

1. Preheat a water bath by setting the sous vide circulator to 140°F (60°C).

2. Mix together the chopped rosemary, 2 tablespoons brown sugar, pepper, and 1 teaspoon of the salt to make your rub.

3. Apply the extra-virgin olive oil on the pork loin, then liberally apply rub to all sides.

4. Place the pork in a vacuum-seal bag or zip-top bag.

5. Mix together the sliced apples, lemon juice, butter, remaining brown sugar, remaining salt, cinnamon, nutmeg, and vanilla.

6. Place the apple mixture in a vacuum-seal bag or zip-top bag.

7. Place just the pork in the preheated water bath (use the immersion technique on page 23 if you are using a zip-top bag), and set the timer for 6 hours.

8. After 4 hours, add the bag with the apple mixture to bath (use the immersion technique if you are using a zip-top bag).

FINISHING STEPS

9. Twenty minutes before the timer goes off, light charcoal for direct cooking, or preheat a gas grill.

10. Remove the pork loin roast from the bag and blot with a dry paper towel.

11. Apply a small amount of vegetable oil to the outside of the roast, then grill all sides over direct heat, 5–10 minutes.

12. After pork is seared, remove from heat and allow to rest, 5–10 minutes.

13. While pork rests, heat a cast-iron skillet over direct heat and add the apple mixture directly from the bag.

14. Heat apples, turning frequently until the liquid has been reduced to a syrup and the apples become caramelized.

15. Slice the pork loin into ½-inch-thick slices and serve topped with apple mixture.

16. Enjoy!

CHAR SIU GRILLED PORK RIBS

Chinese-style pork ribs are savory, sticky, and sweet, with those Chinese spices taking you into flavor overload. You and your guests will absolutely love these!

PREP TIME: 30–40 minutes **COOK TIME:** 8 hours sous vide, plus 5–10 minutes on grill
SERVES: 7–14

1 cup hoisin sauce
½ cup mirin
½ cup honey
½ cup soy sauce
2 tablespoons ketchup
2 tablespoons Chinese hot chili paste
2 tablespoons fresh grated ginger

2 tablespoons dehydrated onion
3 cloves garlic, finely minced
2 teaspoons rice vinegar
2 teaspoons red food coloring (optional)
1–2 racks pork spareribs, trimmed St. Louis style
1–2 chopped fresh green onion, to garnish

1. Preheat a water bath by setting the sous vide circulator to 165°F (73.9°C).

2. In a medium bowl, mix all of the ingredients except for the meat and green onion, and set aside.

3. Remove the membrane on the back of the rib rack.

4. Reserve half of the sauce for the final cook and then baste ribs.

5. Place the ribs in a vacuum-seal bag or zip-top bag.

6. Immerse the ribs in the water bath (use the immersion technique on page 23 if you are using a zip-top bag), and set the timer for 8 hours.

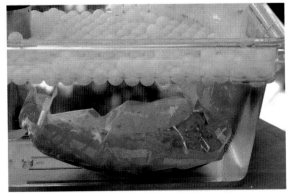

FINISHING STEPS

7. Twenty minutes before the timer goes off, light charcoal for direct cooking, or preheat a gas grill.

8. Remove the ribs from the bag and blot with a dry paper towel.

9. Baste the ribs with the reserved BBQ sauce.

10. Grill the ribs over direct heat on both sides until glaze sets and char marks appear, 5–10 minutes.

11. Allow the ribs to rest for 5 minutes, slice, and garnish with chopped fresh green onion.

St. Louis Style

If trimming St. Louis style, locate the longest bone in the rack. Make an incision at the top of the rib, then follow the seam of fat across the rack, to the top of the shortest rib bone. Trim off any loose-hanging flaps of meat.

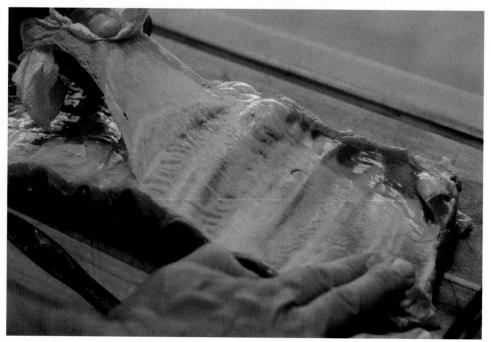

TACOS AL PASTOR

Another of my favorite Mexican street foods, al pastor cooked the traditional way requires a vertical grill burner set at a low temperature. The thin, marinated pork slices are stacked high on the vertical spit and topped with fresh pineapple for a delicious, savory result with a slightly sweet caramel exterior from the dripping pineapple juices. You can simulate this specialized dish very effectively by using sous vide and your grill!

PREP TIME: 20 minutes, plus 8–12 hours to marinate **COOK TIME:** 24 hours sous vide, plus 30–45 minutes on grill **SERVES:** 10 (2 tacos per person)

½ white onion, quartered
¾ cup pineapple juice, divided
½ cup fresh orange juice
¼ cup white vinegar
4 cloves garlic
1 teaspoon ground cumin

2 teaspoons adobo paste
¼ cup chili powder
2 teaspoons dry Mexican oregano
1 (4- to 8-pound) boneless pork shoulder
1 whole pineapple
20 street taco–size corn tortillas

TOPPINGS:

chopped fresh cilantro
¼ chopped white onion
Cotija cheese

salsa
1–2 small limes, cut into wedges

1. Place the onion, ½ cup of pineapple juice, orange juice, vinegar, garlic, cumin, adobo paste, chili powder, and oregano in a blender or food processor, and blend into a liquid.

2. Place the pork shoulder in a large zip-top bag or a glass bowl. Pour the marinade over the meat, ensuring that it is fully covered.

3. Place the pork in the refrigerator and marinate for 8–12 hours.

4. Remove the pork from the bag and shake off excess marinade over the sink.

5. Preheat a water bath by setting the sous vide circulator to 165°F (73.9°C).

6. Place the pork shoulder in a vacuum-seal bag or zip-top bag.

7. Immerse the pork in the water bath (use the immersion technique on page 23 if you are using a zip-top bag), and set the timer for 24 hours.

FINISHING STEPS

8. Thirty to forty minutes prior to removing pork from the sous vide bath, preheat grill to 350°F (176.7°C), and peel pineapple, leaving crown to use as a handle while grilling.

9. Remove the pork from the bag and blot with a dry paper towel.

10. Place the pork shoulder on the grill over indirect heat, and baste with the remaining pineapple juice.

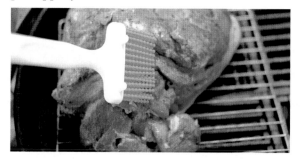

11. Place lid (or close lid) on cooker. If using a kettle-type charcoal cooker, make sure the lid vent is over the meat. This creates a convection oven effect.

12. Remove the pork shoulder from the grill when a reddish mahogany color develops and the pineapple juice sets. This should take 30–40 minutes. Let the pork rest 5–10 minutes while you grill the pineapple.

13. Place the peeled pineapple on the grill and cook all sides until softened, 5–10 minutes.

14. The pork will be very tender now. Pull it apart with two forks or gloved hands and chop the pineapple into small pieces.

15. Mix the pork and pineapple together in pan.

16. Heat tortillas on grill, or in pan. Add the meat to each tortilla and garnish with chopped cilantro and onion, topping with Cotija cheese, salsa, and a squeeze of fresh lime.

MAPLE-GLAZED PORK BELLY, LETTUCE, TOMATO, AND AVOCADO SANDWICH

Who doesn't like a good BLT? With this recipe, we're taking the BLT up several notches, turning this simple sammie into something very special!

PREP TIME: 20 minutes   **COOK TIME:** 8 hours sous vide, plus 4–5 minutes on grill   **SERVES:** 4–5

⅛ cup maple syrup
1 (2- to 4-pound) pork belly, skin removed
8–10 slices quality bread

coarse-ground kosher or sea salt, to taste
fresh ground pepper, to taste

TOPPINGS:
mayo
1–2 sliced tomatoes

1–2 sliced avocados
green lettuce

1. Preheat a water bath by setting the sous vide circulator to 155°F (68.3°C).

2. Brush a thin layer of maple syrup on all sides of the pork belly.

3. Sprinkle on a very light amount of kosher or sea salt.

4. Place the pork belly in a vacuum-seal bag or zip-top bag.

5. Immerse the pork belly in a water bath (use the immersion technique on page 23 if you are using a zip-top bag), and set the timer for 8 hours.

FINISHING STEPS

6. Twenty minutes before the timer goes off, light charcoal for direct cooking, or preheat a gas grill.

7. Remove the pork belly from the bag and blot with a dry paper towel.

8. Season with just a little more salt and fresh ground pepper.

9. Grill both sides over direct heat for about 2 minutes per side, or until a nice color develops.

10. Grill the bread slices over direct heat, on both sides, until desired doneness is achieved.

11. Slice the pork belly into ¼-inch-thick slices.

12. Build the first sandwich by spreading mayo on both slices of bread and layering on the pork belly, tomato, avocado and lettuce. Repeat for remaining sandwiches.

CUBAN GRILLED BONELESS PORK LOIN CHOPS

This recipe is based on a very traditional Cuban mojo, which is a savory blend of citrus, herbs, and spices. This marinade can be used on a variety of pork dishes. It also makes an amazing injection for large cuts, such as shoulder or even whole hog.

PREP TIME: 20 minutes, plus 12–24 hours to marinate   **COOK TIME:** 2 hours sous vide, plus 2–4 minutes on grill   **SERVES:** 2–4

1 cup sour orange juice (or substitute ¾ cup orange juice, 2 tablespoons lemon juice, 2 tablespoons lime juice)

1 tablespoon dried Mexican or Italian oregano

4 dried bay leaves

1 bulb garlic, peeled and smashed

1 teaspoon ground cumin

4 teaspoons course ground kosher or sea salt, plus more to taste

¼ cup pineapple juice

2–4 (6- to 8-ounce) boneless pork loin chops

1. Mix the first 7 ingredients together in a large glass bowl and reserve ¼ cup for basting on the grill.

2. Place the pork loin chops in the bowl. Cover and refrigerate for 12–24 hours.

3. Preheat a water bath by setting the sous vide circulator to 140°F (60°C).

4. Remove the pork from the marinade and gently shake off excess liquid.

5. Place the pork in a vacuum-seal bag or zip-top bag.

6. Immerse the pork chops in the water bath (use the immersion on page 23 technique if you are using a zip-top bag), and set the timer for 2 hours.

FINISHING STEPS

7. Twenty minutes before the timer goes off, light charcoal for direct cooking, or preheat a gas grill.

8. Remove the pork chops from the bag and blot with a dry paper towel.

9. Season with a little salt if desired.

10. Grill the meat over direct heat for about 1 minute per side, basting each side with reserved marinade.

11. Serve with traditional side dishes, which include rice, black beans, and fried plantains.

GRILLED PORK STEAKS ADOBO

This recipe is my take on Filipino-style pork adobo. Adobo is just one of those simple seasonings that comes to life during the cook. This marinade isn't just for pork, by the way. Try this on beef and chicken, too!

PREP TIME: 20 minutes, plus 45 minutes to marinate **COOK TIME:** 2 hours sous vide, plus 2–4 minutes on grill **SERVES:** 2–4

3 tablespoons vegetable oil
4 cloves garlic, chopped
½ cup soy sauce
½ cup white vinegar
2 bay leaves
1 teaspoon ground black pepper

1 cup water
2 tablespoons honey
2–4 pork shoulder steaks
coarse-ground kosher or sea salt, to taste
1 tablespoon olive oil

1. Mix the first 8 ingredients together in a large glass bowl, reserving ¼ cup for later use.

2. Preheat a water bath by setting the sous vide circulator to 140°F (60°C).

3. Marinate the pork steaks in the bowl for 45 minutes to 1 hour, covered, in the refrigerator.

4. Remove the pork steaks from the marinade and gently shake off excess liquid.

5. Place the steaks in a vacuum-seal bag or zip-top bag.

6. Immerse the pork steaks in the water bath (use the immersion technique on page 23 if you are using a zip-top bag), and set the timer for 2 hours.

FINISHING STEPS

7. Twenty minutes before the timer goes off, light charcoal for direct cooking, or preheat a gas grill.

8. Remove the pork steaks from the bag and blot with a dry paper towel.

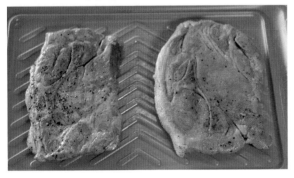

9. Season with a little salt.

10. Grill the steaks over direct heat for about 1 minute per side, basting with reserved marinade.

11. Serve with white rice and enjoy!

PEPPER-CRUSTED BONELESS PORK TENDERLOIN

This very tasty loin cut gets a bad rap because of how difficult it is to cook properly. Using traditional means can easily result in disaster, while using the sous vide method is foolproof. Believe me!

PREP TIME: 20 minutes   **COOK TIME:** 3 hours sous vide, plus 15–20 minutes on grill   **SERVES:** 6–8

1 (2- to 3-pound) pork tenderloin

3 tablespoons olive oil, divided

3 tablespoons freshly ground black pepper

3–4 sprigs fresh thyme

coarse-ground kosher or sea salt, to taste

1. Preheat a water bath by setting the sous vide circulator to 135°F (57°C).

2. Brush the pork tenderloin with a light coating of olive oil, then a healthy coating of black pepper.

3. Place the tenderloin in a vacuum-seal bag or zip-top bag, along with the thyme.

4. Immerse the tenderloin in the water bath (use the immersion technique on page 23 if you are using a zip-top bag), and set the timer for 3 hours.

FINISHING STEPS

5. Twenty minutes before the timer goes off, light charcoal for indirect cooking, or preheat a gas grill.

6. Remove the tenderloin from the bag and blot with a dry paper towel.

7. Place the pork on grill set up for indirect heat. Coat with a thin layer of olive oil, then season with salt. Close the lid on the grill; if using a charcoal grill, be sure that the lid vent is over the food. This will cause convection cooking.

8. After grilling for 1–2 minutes per side and the desired crust has developed, remove the pork from the grill and allow 10 minutes to rest.

9. Slice and serve.

CITRUS GINGER PORK CHOPS

Asian influenced and packed with flavor, this is one of my personal favorites. The marinade also goes great with chicken, by the way.

PREP TIME: 30-40 minutes, plus 4-8 hours to marinate   **COOK TIME:** 2 hours sous vide, plus 2-4 minutes on grill   **SERVES:** 3-4

½ cup fresh orange juice
¼ cup fresh lemon juice
3 tablespoons soy sauce
1 tablespoon minced ginger
1 teaspoon minced garlic

1½ teaspoons Asian chili sauce
zest of one orange
zest of one small lemon
½ teaspoon salt
3-4 pork chops

1. Mix all of the ingredients except the pork chops together in a non-metallic bowl.

2. Place the chops in the bowl, assuring that they are coated with the marinade. Cover and refrigerate for 4-8 hours.

3. Preheat a water bath by setting the sous vide circulator to 140°F (60°C).

4. Place the chops in a vacuum-seal bag or zip-top bag.

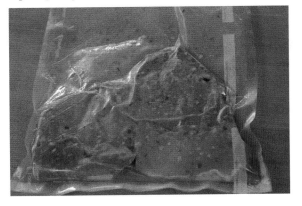

5. Immerse the chops in the water bath (use the immersion technique on page 23 if you are using a zip-top bag), and set the timer for 2 hours.

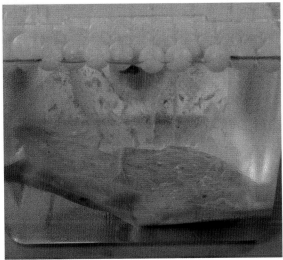

FINISHING STEPS

6. Twenty minutes before the timer goes off, light charcoal for direct cooking, or preheat a gas grill.

7. Remove the chops from the bag and blot with a dry paper towel. Try not to wipe off the zest or bits of ginger and garlic.

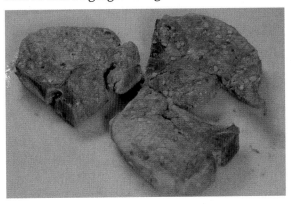

8. Grill the chops over direct heat for 1–2 minutes on each side, until nice char marks appear.

9. Allow the chops to rest for 5 minutes prior to serving. Enjoy!

SOUTHERN-STYLE SMOKED PORK CHOPS

Every time I cook pork chops, I hear Bobby Brady's voice uttering, "Pork chops and apple sauce for supper" in a very poorly executed Humphrey Bogart impersonation. As I type this, I realize that I totally just dated myself! Oh, well! Smoked pork chops rock, and I think Bobby would approve.

PREP TIME: 15 minutes   **COOK TIME:** 2 hours sous vide, plus 1 hour on smoker   **SERVES:** 2

AP Rub #1 (page 19) or #2 (page 20), about 1 teaspoon per side, per chop

2 (10-ounce) bone-in pork chops

1. Preheat a water bath by setting the sous vide circulator to 130°F (54.5°C).

2. Coat the chops liberally with the AP Rub of your choice.

3. Place the chops in vacuum-seal bags or zip-top bags.

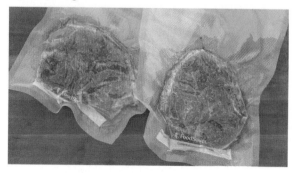

4. Immerse the chops in the water bath (use the immersion technique on page 23 if you are using zip-top bags), and set the timer for 2 hours.

FINISHING STEPS

5. Preheat your smoker to 250°F (121.1°C), or set up your grill for indirect heat. For this cook I used a ceramic Kamado grill.

6. Remove the chops from the bags and blot off excess liquid with a dry paper towel. Apply more rub if needed and place the chops on the cooker.

8. Remove the chops from the smoker and allow to rest for 5–10 minutes before serving.

7. Smoke pork using a wood, such as pecan or apple, for 1 hour to add a nice, smoky flavor.

Poultry

HULI-HULI CHICKEN

Huli-huli literally means "turn-turn." This Hawaiian favorite is prepared by grilling a chicken over mesquite wood and basting it with a sweet island-inspired sauce.

PREP TIME: 20 minutes **COOK TIME:** 3 hours sous vide, plus 10–20 minutes on grill **SERVES:** 2–4

¾ cup soy sauce
¾ cup packed brown sugar
¾ cup ketchup
2 tablespoons red wine vinegar

2½ teaspoons fresh minced ginger
6 cloves garlic, crushed
1 (2- to 3-pound) chicken, cut in half
coarse-ground kosher or sea salt, to taste

1. Preheat a water bath by setting the sous vide circulator to 146°F (63.3°C).

2. Mix the soy sauce, brown sugar, ketchup, red wine vinegar, ginger, and garlic together in a large glass bowl. Reserve half the marinade for basting during the grilling process.

3. Brush both chicken halves, front and back, with marinade. This will get that huli-huli flavor into the skin and flesh of the bird. Place the halves in vacuum-seal bags or zip-top bags.

4. Immerse the chicken in the water bath (use the immersion technique on page 23 if you are using zip-top bags), and set the timer for 3 hours.

FINISHING STEPS

5. Twenty minutes before the timer goes off, light charcoal, or preheat a gas grill, for direct and indirect heat.

6. Remove the chicken from the bags and blot with a dry paper towel. Season with a little salt.

7. Place the chicken over indirect heat. Coat both sides with a thin layer of the reserved marinade. Close the lid on the grill; if using a charcoal grill, be sure that the lid vent is over the food. This will cause convection cooking, rendering the fat underneath the skin and caramelizing the sauce.

8. After 5–10 minutes, the sauce should start to set. The next step will be moving the chicken to grill over direct heat. This will really set the sauce, creating a wonderful sticky glaze and slight char. Make sure you turn-turn so it doesn't burn! Once the desired color and texture has been reached, remove from the grill and allow to rest 5–10 minutes.

9. Slice and serve.

CRISPY BALSAMIC SEARED DUCK BREAST

Seared duck breast...wow! So rich and decadent, and guess what? It tastes like beef fillet! This is one of my personal favorites, but duck breast isn't cheap. By going with sous vide, you'll have guaranteed results.

PREP TIME: 5 minutes   **COOK TIME:** 2 hours sous vide, plus 2 minutes on griddle.   **SERVES:** 2–4

2–4 boneless, skin-on duck breasts

5 tablespoons balsamic vinegar, plus extra for drizzling

coarse-ground kosher or sea salt, to taste

freshly ground black pepper, to taste

2 tablespoons peanut or canola oil

1. Preheat water bath by setting the sous vide circulator to 130°F (54.4°C).

2. With a sharp knife, score the skin on the duck breasts in a crisscross pattern, being careful not to penetrate the flesh.

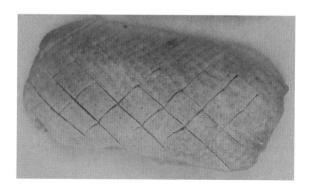

3. Brush the breasts, front and back, with balsamic vinegar.

4. Place breasts in vacuum-seal bags or zip-top bags.

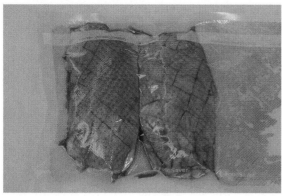

5. Immerse the duck breasts in the water bath (use the immersion technique on page 23 if you are using zip-top bags), and set the timer for 2 hours.

FINISHING STEPS

6. Twenty minutes before the timer goes off, light charcoal for direct cooking, or preheat a gas grill.

7. Remove the breasts from the bag and blot with a dry paper towel. Season with a little kosher or sea salt and ground black pepper.

9. Place duck breasts skin-side down on the hot griddle, pushing down with your fingers or spatula to ensure that all of the skin surface comes in contact with the hot griddle or skillet.

10. Flip after about 1 minute and sear non-skin side another minute.

8. Preheat a griddle or cast-iron skillet over direct heat. Add a couple tablespoons of a cooking oil with a high smoke point, such as peanut oil or canola oil.

11. Remove from the grill and allow 5–10 minutes to rest. Slice and serve with a little balsamic vinegar drizzled over the top.

POLLO ASADO (MEXICAN-STYLE GRILLED CHICKEN)

Pollo asado is Mexican-style marinated grilled chicken. The seasoning can vary in any number of ways, depending on what region of Mexico the recipe comes from. I live in San Diego, California, and our Mexican food is heavily influenced by the small towns on the Baja coast.

PREP TIME: 45 minutes, plus 2 hours to marinate on grill   **SERVES:** 4-6

COOK TIME: 2 hours sous vide, plus 4-5 minutes

2 tablespoons ground ancho chili powder

2 teaspoons dried oregano (use Mexican if you can get it)

1 teaspoon ground cumin

¼ teaspoon ground cloves

½ teaspoon ground cinnamon

6 cloves garlic, peeled, smashed, and minced

¼ cup apple cider vinegar

¼ cup orange juice

¼ cup lime juice

1 fryer chicken, cut up

coarse-ground kosher or sea salt, to taste

freshly ground black pepper, to taste

1. Mix together all of the ingredients except the chicken in a non-metallic bowl.

2. Place the chicken pieces in the bowl, assuring that they have been completely coated with the marinade. Cover and place in the refrigerator for 2 hours.

3. Preheat a water bath by setting the sous vide circulator to 146°F (63.3°C).

4. Place the chicken in vacuum-seal bags or zip-top bags.

5. Immerse the chicken in the water bath (use the immersion technique on page 23 if you are using zip-top bags), and set the timer for 2 hours.

FINISHING STEPS

6. Twenty minutes before the timer goes off, light charcoal for direct cooking, or preheat a gas grill.

7. Remove the chicken pieces from the bag and blot with a dry paper towel. Season with a little kosher or sea salt and ground black pepper.

8. Sear the chicken over medium-high direct heat, flipping frequently as to not burn the skin. You're looking for the skin to tighten up and develop nice grill marks, which should develop within 1–2 minutes per side.

9. Remove from the grill and allow 5–10 minutes to rest. Serve with beans, rice, and warm tortillas to keep this meal legit!

TANDOORI-SEASONED CHICKEN (WITHOUT THE TANDOOR)

The flavors of this dish were heavily influenced by tandoori chicken and chicken tikka. This isn't quite as spicy as the real deal, but you'll still get that authentic Indian cuisine feeling from it.

PREP TIME: 30 minutes, plus 2 hours to marinate grill **SERVES:** 4–8

COOK TIME: 2 sous vide, plus 4–5 minutes on

1½ cups plain Greek yogurt

1½ tablespoons lemon juice

1½ teaspoons freshly ground black pepper, plus more to taste

1½ teaspoons ground cayenne pepper

1½ teaspoons ground cinnamon

1½ teaspoons ground cumin

1 tablespoon smashed and minced fresh ginger

1 teaspoon coarse-ground kosher or sea salt, plus more to taste

4 chicken legs

4 chicken thighs

1. Mix together all of the ingredients except the chicken in a non-metallic bowl.

2. Place the chicken pieces in the bowl, assuring that they are completely coated with the yogurt marinade. Cover and place in the refrigerator for 2 hours.

3. Preheat a water bath by setting the sous vide circulator to 146°F (63.3°C).

4. Place the chicken pieces in vacuum-seal bags or zip-top bags.

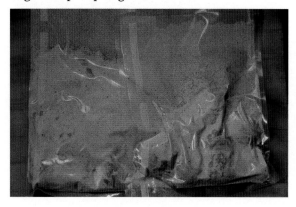

5. Immerse the chicken in the water bath (use the immersion technique on page 23 if you are using zip-top bags), and set the timer for 2 hours.

FINISHING STEPS

6. Twenty minutes before the timer goes off, light charcoal for direct cooking, or preheat a gas grill.

7. Remove the chicken pieces from the bag and lightly blot with a dry paper towel. Season with a little kosher or sea salt and ground black pepper.

8. Sear the chicken on your grill over medium-high direct heat, flipping frequently so as to not burn the skin. The skin will start to tighten up and grill marks will develop.

9. Remove from the grill and allow 5–10 minutes to rest. Best served with saffron rice, veggies, and warm flatbread.

BBQ (SMOKED) CHICKEN

Chicken on a smoker can be a little tricky. If not done correctly, you can end up with an over-smoked bird sporting rubbery skin. Not a great combo! The nice thing about starting out with sous vide is the meat will be done perfectly—juicy and tender, with deep flavor from the barbecue rub. Plus, you'll need less time in the smoker, and you can cook at a hotter temperature, so the rubbery skin issue is no more!

PREP TIME: 30 minutes   **COOK TIME:** 3 hours sous vide, plus 45–60 minutes on smoker
SERVES: 4–8

½ cup AP Rub #1 (page 19) or AP Rub #2 (page 20)

1 chicken, cut in half
1 tablespoon olive oil

1. Preheat a water bath by setting the sous vide circulator to 150°F (65.6°C).

2. Brush the chicken with a light coating of olive oil, then sprinkle a liberal coating of the AP Rub of your choice, reserving some of the rub for later.

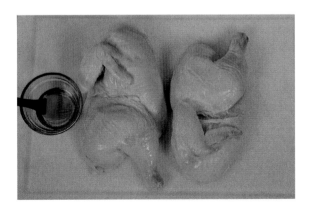

3. Place the chicken halves in vacuum-seal bags or zip-top bags.

4. Immerse the chicken in the water bath (use the immersion technique on page 23 if you are using zip-top bags), and set the timer for 3 hours.

FINISHING STEPS

5. Preheat your smoker to 300°F (148.9°C), adding the cooking wood of your choice.

6. Remove the chicken pieces from the bag and lightly blot with a dry paper towel. Apply a little more BBQ rub.

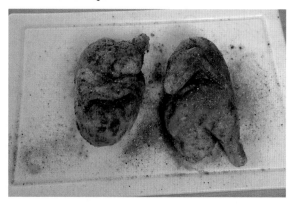

7. Place the chicken in the smoker and cook until the skin tightens up and desired color is achieved, 45 minutes to 1 hour.

8. Remove from the smoker and allow 10–15 minutes to rest before cutting up and serving.

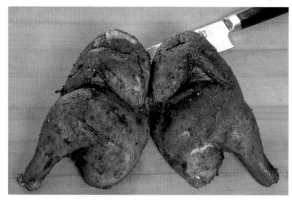

CEDAR-PLANK CHICKEN BREAST

Okay, first off, you're cooking on top of a plank of wood. How cool is that! The thing I really like about plank cooking is how easy it is. Follow a couple of basic steps and even the novice outdoor cook can put out perfect food "planking."

PREP TIME: 1 hour   **COOK TIME:** 3 hours sous vide, plus 15–20 minutes on grill   **SERVES:** 2–4

olive oil
2–4 chicken breasts, bone in and skin on

2–4 tablespoons lemon pepper
coarse-ground kosher or sea salt, to taste

1. Soak the plank(s) in water for 1 hour.

2. Preheat a water bath by setting the sous vide circulator to 146°F (63.3°C).

3. Brush a light coating of olive oil on the chicken breasts, then season both skin and bone sides with lemon pepper.

4. Place the chicken breasts in vacuum-seal bags or zip-top bags.

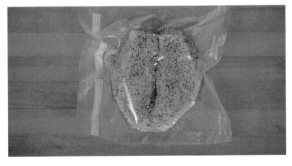

5. Immerse the chicken in the water bath (use the immersion technique on page 23 if you are using zip-top bags), and set the timer for 3 hours.

FINISHING STEPS

6. Twenty minutes before the timer goes off, light charcoal for direct cooking, or preheat a gas grill.

7. Place the cedar planks over direct heat until you start hearing the wood "pop," 1–2 minutes. This both preheats and sanitizes the cooking surface. Flip the planks over and center them in the grill.

8. Remove the chicken pieces from the bag and lightly blot with a dry paper towel. Season with a little salt. Place on top of the planks.

9. Close the lid on your cooker, with the vent about halfway open. Cook until the skin tightens and the desired color is achieved, 15–20 minutes.

10. Remove from the grill and allow 10–15 minutes to rest before cutting up and serving.

TURKEY SKILLET STEW

This hearty dish is an entire meal! So warm and filling. Bring your knife and fork to the party.

PREP TIME: 30 minutes   **COOK TIME:** 24 hours sous vide, plus 40 minutes on grill   **SERVES:** 2-4

2-4 turkey thighs, bone-in, skin-on
1 pat of butter per thigh
4-6 sprigs fresh thyme
4-6 sprigs fresh sage
1 onion, diced
4-8 cloves garlic
15 baby carrots

15 baby potatoes
2 stalks celery, chopped
coarse-ground kosher or sea salt, to taste
cooking oil, to coat cast-iron skillet
freshly ground black pepper, to taste
1 cup chicken broth

1. Preheat a water bath by setting the sous vide circulator to 158°F (70°C).

2. Place the turkey in vacuum-seal or zip-top bags along with a pat of butter on each side and the fresh herbs. Place vegetables in a separate bag.

3. Immerse the turkey and vegetables in the water bath (use the immersion technique on page 23 if you are using zip-top bags), and set the timer for 24 hours.

4. Remove the turkey and vegetables from the bags. Blot turkey with dry paper towel and season with salt and pepper.

FINISHING STEPS

5. Set up a cooker for indirect heat and preheat to 350°F (176.7°C) along with a large cast-iron skillet prior to the timer going off.

6. Once preheated, coat the inside of the skillet with just a little cooking oil. Add the turkey thighs, skin-side down, and press them on the meat side with your hands or a spatula. This will assure a good sear and crisp skin.

7. After the skin is seared, flip the thighs and pour in the chicken broth. Surround the thighs with the cooked vegetables. Add salt to taste and close the lid on the cooker.

8. After about 40 minutes, when the broth has reduced and vegetables have become tender, remove from cooker and allow to rest 15–20 minutes.

9. Serve with bread, butter, and a knife and fork!

SOCAL CHICKEN CLUB SUB

Boneless, skinless chicken breast is probably the most basic poultry choice out there, yet many people struggle with cooking it. Quite often, the breasts turn out dry and tough as shoe leather. Why? Fat, skin, and bones help protect meat from drying out during the cooking process. Kiss that problem goodbye!

PREP TIME: 20 minutes   **COOK TIME:** 2 hours sous vide, plus 8 minutes on grill   **SERVES:** 1–3

½ cup mayo

¼ cup chipotle sauce

1 teaspoon onion powder

1 teaspoon garlic powder

1 teaspoon paprika

½ teaspoon ground cinnamon

½ teaspoon freshly ground black pepper

2 (5–6 ounce) boneless, skinless chicken breasts

2 teaspoons olive oil

2 teaspoons cooking oil

coarse-ground kosher or sea salt, to taste

2 slices bacon, halved

1 flute sourdough bread

TOPPINGS:

1 red onion, thinly sliced

1 avocado, sliced

mixed greens (baby arugula and baby spinach)

1 tomato, thinly sliced

Monterey Jack cheese

1. Preheat a water bath by setting the sous vide circulator to 146°F (63.3°C).

2. Mix the mayo and chipotle together, and place in the refrigerator until needed.

3. Mix the onion powder, garlic powder, paprika, cinnamon, and black pepper together in a bowl.

4. Brush the chicken breast with a light coating of olive oil, then season with the rub mixture.

5. Place the chicken breasts in vacuum-seal bags or zip-top bags.

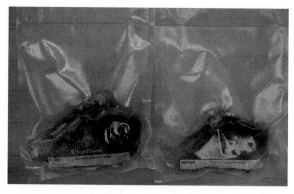

6. Immerse the chicken in the water bath (use the immersion technique on page 23 if you are using zip-top bags), and set the timer for 2 hours.

FINISHING STEPS

7. Twenty minutes before the timer goes off, light charcoal for direct cooking, or preheat a gas grill.

8. Remove chicken breasts from the bags, drain, and blot with a dry paper towel. Apply a light coating of cooking oil and season with salt to taste.

9. Out at the grill, cook the bacon in a skillet or on a griddle until crisp, 5–7 minutes.

10. Sear the breasts over direct heat until nice grill marks have developed and meat has tightened a bit. This should only take 1–2 minutes per side.

11. Slice the chicken breasts in ¼-inch-thick, easy-to-eat pieces.

12. Build your sandwich as you like. I spread on the chipotle mayo on both sides of the roll and then layer on all of the goodness!

JAMAICAN JERK CHICKEN

My wife and I spent our honeymoon in Jamaica and we absolutely fell in love with jerk chicken. It is such a fragrant, spicy hot, savory, and smoky dish all at the same time. Every time I prepare this, the smells bring us back to the island.

Jerk chicken not only gets its flavor from the wonderful spices and seasonings that go into the paste, but the pimento wood that it is cooked over. I have come up with a clever way of simulating the unique flavor that the Jamaican pimento produces.

Also, if you can find them, use scotch bonnet peppers. Both habanero and scotch bonnet are extremely hot peppers! I suggest removing the seeds and white membrane before using them.

PREP TIME: 1 hour, plus 12-24 hours to marinate   **COOK TIME:** 4 hours sous vide, plus 30-40 to simmer sauce and 20 minutes on grill   **SERVES:** 2-6

1 whole fryer chicken, cut in half

handful whole, dried allspice berries (as smoke source)

fresh lime wedges, to serve

FOR THE PASTE:
2 teaspoons ground allspice
⅔ cup packed brown sugar
8 cloves garlic
1–3 habanero peppers or scotch bonnet, depending on desired heat level
1 tablespoon ground thyme

1 bunch green onions (about 6 bulbs)
1 teaspoon ground cinnamon
½ teaspoon ground nutmeg
1 teaspoon coarse-ground kosher or sea salt
1 teaspoon freshly ground black pepper
2 tablespoons dark soy sauce

FOR THE SAUCE:
2 tablespoons jerk paste (above)
1 cup lager beer

½ cup pineapple juice
½ cup ketchup

1. Put all of the ingredients for the paste in a food processor or blender and liquefy.

2. Reserve 2 tablespoons of paste, then thoroughly rub the remaining paste all over the chicken halves, completely covering the skin and cavity areas.

3. Place coated chicken halves in vacuum-seal bags or zip-top bags, and place in refrigerator overnight to marinate.

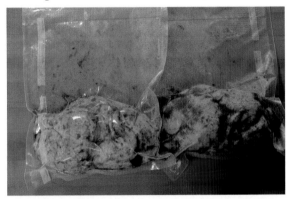

4. Prepare the sauce by mixing 2 tablespoons of the paste with the beer, pineapple juice, and ketchup. Simmer on the stovetop until sauce reduces and thickens, 30–40 minutes.

5. Preheat a water bath by setting the sous vide circulator to 149°F (63.9°C).

6. Immerse the sealed chicken in the water bath (use the immersion technique on page 23 if you are using zip-top bags), and set the timer for 4 hours.

FINISHING STEPS

7. Preheat your grill for indirect heat. If using a charcoal grill, place a good amount of charcoal on just one side of the grill, and adjust dampers targeting 375°F–400°F as your cooking temperature.

8. Jamaican pimento wood is actually allspice. So, sprinkle a small handful of whole dried allspice berries directly onto the burning charcoal. If using a gas grill, you can place the berries in a small foil pan, directly over the burners.

9. Place the chicken halves on the side of the grill opposite of the heat source. Make sure that the breasts are facing away from the heat.

10. Thoroughly brush the chicken with jerk sauce and close the lid on the grill. You want the skin to tighten up and the sauce to begin to form a sticky glaze. This should take 15 minutes or so.

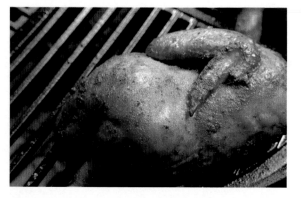

11. For that authentic look and taste, it's time to give the chicken just a little bit of char. Carefully grill both sides of the chicken halves directly over the burning charcoal. It will only take 1 minute or so to produce nice grill marks on both sides.

12. Remove from the grill and allow 5–10 minutes to rest. Serve with fresh lime wedges and your favorite sides.

SPICED RUM GRILLED CHICKEN WINGS

Dark rum has a slightly sweet caramel flavor that plays very nicely in a variety of sauces. The sauce used in this recipe starts out like a refreshing cocktail and is perfect on chicken.

PREP TIME: 30 minutes, plus 4–8 hours to marinate   **COOK TIME:** 2 hours sous vide, plus 2–5 minutes on grill   **SERVES:** 4–8

¾ cup dark rum

½ cup pineapple juice

3 tablespoons soy sauce

1–2 habanero chili peppers, seeded and minced

1 tablespoon minced fresh ginger

1 teaspoon Chinese five spice

1 teaspoon pickling spice

2 tablespoons packed brown sugar

6–12 chicken wings, tips removed and cut into drumettes and flats

1 teaspoon coarse-ground kosher or sea salt

1. In a large glass bowl, mix together the rum, pineapple juice, soy sauce, habanero, ginger, five spice, and pickling spice, and allow the liquid to soften up the spices for about 10 minutes before adding the brown sugar. Mix well and reserve ⅓ cup for later use as a glaze.

2. Pour the reserved liquid into a saucepan and bring to a boil. Reduce heat and allow to simmer until reduced to ¼ cup.

3. Place the chicken in the bowl with marinade, cover with plastic, and refrigerate for at least 4 hours.

4. Preheat a water bath by setting the sous vide circulator to 146°F (63.3°C).

5. Remove the chicken from the marinade and place in vacuum-seal bags or zip-top bags.

6. Immerse the chicken in the water bath (use the immersion technique on page 23 if you are using zip-top bags), and set the timer for 2 hours.

FINISHING STEPS

7. Twenty minutes before the timer goes off, light charcoal for indirect cooking, or preheat a gas grill.

8. Remove the chicken pieces from the bag and allow excess liquid to fall from the wings.

9. Place chicken wings on the indirect side of the grill, but close to the center. This will provide a good searing heat, without the risk of flare-ups. Baste the wings with the reduced marinade.

10. Grill the wings until nice grill marks appear and the sauce becomes sticky, 1–2 minutes.

11. This is tailgating food. Garnish with a little chopped green onion and serve with napkins!

SMOKED "PTERODACTYL" WINGS (TURKEY WINGS)

These bad boys don't get enough attention, in my opinion. One wing can feed one person, and they are so tasty. After the holidays is the best time to find them in the meat department of your local store.

PREP TIME: 15 minutes   **COOK TIME:** 2 hours sous vide, plus 1 hour on smoker   **SERVES:** 4

4 whole turkey wings

¼ cup AP Rub #1 (page 19) or AP Rub #2 (page 20).

1. Preheat water bath by setting the sous vide circulator to 150°F (65.6°C).

2. Coat the wings liberally with the AP Rub of your choice.

3. Place the wings in vacuum-seal bags or zip-top bags.

4. Immerse the wings in the water bath (use the water immersion technique on page 23 if you are using zip-top bags), and set the timer for 2 hours.

FINISHING STEPS

5. Preheat your smoker between 275°F (107.2°C) and 300°F (148.9°C), or set up your grill for indirect heat. I like to go closer to 300°F with poultry to avoid rubbery skin.

6. Remove the wings from the bags and blot off excess liquid with a dry paper towel. Apply more rub if needed.

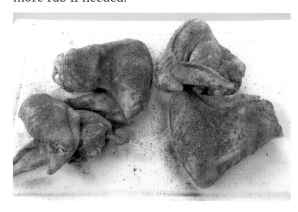

7. Smoke wings using a mild wood, such as pecan, almond, or maple, for 1 hour to tighten up that skin and add a wonderful smoky flavor.

8. Remove the wings from the smoker and allow to rest for 5–10 minutes before serving.

Lamb

GRILLED RACK OF LAMB

Rack of lamb is meat royalty. Such a beautiful cut that just screams class and is a real showstopper during the holidays! Now, a full rack of lamb isn't cheap, and this can put a little pressure on the home cook. Combining sous vide and the grill will not only give you the perfect cook, but a moment you'll be proud to share.

PREP TIME: 30 minutes   **COOK TIME:** 3 hours sous vide, plus 5–8 minutes on grill   **SERVES:** 4–8

1 ½- to 2-pound rack of lamb
1 tablespoon olive oil
2–4 teaspoons crushed red pepper
4 cloves garlic, minced
6 slices fresh lemon

4–6 sprigs fresh thyme
4–6 sprigs fresh oregano
canola oil, for brushing
coarse-ground kosher or sea salt, to taste

1. Preheat a water bath by setting the sous vide circulator to 135°F (57.2°C).

2. Brush a light coating of olive oil on both sides of the rack, season with crushed red pepper and garlic, then place it in your vacuum–seal or zip-top bag. Place 3 slices of lemon on both sides, along with the fresh herbs.

3. Immerse the rack in the water bath (use immersion technique on page 23 if you are using a zip-top bag), and set the timer for 3 hours.

FINISHING STEPS

4. Twenty minutes before the timer goes off, light charcoal for direct cooking, or preheat a gas grill.

5. Remove the rack from the bag and blot with a dry paper towel. Brush on a light coating of canola oil and season with kosher salt.

6. Sear the rack on all sides over direct heat, until a nice crust forms on all sides, 5–8 minutes.

7. Remove rack from grill and allow to rest 10–15 minutes before slicing.

8. Slice chops from rack between the bones. Slice one bone per chop for thin portions, or two bones for thicker chops.

GRILLED LAMB STEAKS

Lamb steaks are packed with wonderful, rich flavor. Just add a few basic seasonings and a little fire, and prepare to be amazed!

PREP TIME: 15 minutes   **COOK TIME:** 2 hours sous vide, plus 2–4 minutes on grill   **SERVES:** 2

2 teaspoons olive oil

2 bone-in lamb steaks

2 teaspoons freshly ground black pepper

2 teaspoons granulated garlic

2 teaspoons dehydrated onion

coarse-ground kosher or sea salt, to taste

1. Preheat a water bath by setting the sous vide circulator to 135°F (57.2°C).

2. Brush a light coating of olive oil on both sides of the steaks and season with black pepper, granulated garlic, and dehydrated onion.

3. Place the steaks in vacuum-seal bags or zip-top bags.

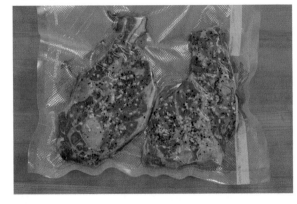

4. Immerse the lamb steaks in the water bath (use the immersion technique on page 23 if you are using zip-top bags), and set the timer for 2 hours.

FINISHING STEPS

5. Twenty minutes before the timer goes off, light charcoal for direct cooking, or preheat a gas grill.

6. Remove the steaks from the bag and blot with a dry paper towel. Season with kosher salt.

7. Sear the steaks over direct heat until nice grill marks form, 2–4 minutes total.

8. Remove the steaks from the grill and allow to rest for 5–10 minutes before serving.

MEDITERRANEAN LAMB KEBABS

The challenge with kebabs is getting them all cooked to the same doneness. Oftentimes when the outdoor cook is grilling up a large number of kebabs, a few are cooked perfectly, some are too rare, while others are burnt to a crisp. This is why sous vide is the perfect call for kebabs!

PREP TIME: 1 hour 30 minutes (includes marinating)   **COOK TIME:** 2 hours sous vide, plus 5 minutes on grill   **SERVES:** 4–8

¾ cup olive oil
½ cup fresh lemon juice
5 cloves garlic, chopped
2 tablespoons chopped fresh mint
1 teaspoon coarse-ground kosher or sea salt
1 teaspoon freshly ground black pepper

1 teaspoon ground coriander
½ teaspoon ground cumin
lemon zest from 1 lemon
2 pounds cubed lamb shoulder meat
1 pound dried apricots
3 medium red onions, each cut into 8 chunks

1. Preheat a water bath by setting the sous vide circulator to 130°F (54.4°C).

2. Combine the olive oil, lemon juice, garlic, mint, salt, pepper, coriander, and cumin, and lemon zest in a bowl and whisk together well. Reserve 1 tablespoons for basting, then add cubed lamb. Cover bowl with plastic wrap and place in the refrigerator for 1 hour.

3. Remove lamb from marinade and thread cubes onto skewers, dividing equally. Thread the apricots and onion chunks alternately on remaining the skewers. Cap the point end of each skewer with an apricot to prevent the sous vide bag from being punctured.

4. Place the kebabs in vacuum-seal bags or zip-top bags.

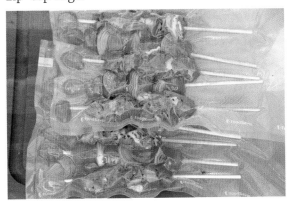

5. Immerse the kebabs in the water bath (use the immersion technique on page 23 if you are using zip-top bags), and set the timer for 2 hours.

FINISHING STEPS

6. Preheat the grill for hot direct heat.

7. Remove the kebabs from the bag and blot off excess liquid with a dry paper towel. Brush each kebab with a little of the reserved marinade.

8. Grill the kebabs over coals, turning them frequently, until a nice sear and grill marks have developed.

9. You can remove the meat, onion, and apricots from the skewers, or leave them intact for a more impressive presentation.

GREEK-STYLE GRILLED LAMB POPS

This is a very simple recipe that explodes with flavor. It is also a very sexy dish that is sure to please the eyes of your guests!

PREP TIME: 30 minutes, plus 1 hour to marinate on grill **SERVES:** 3-6   **COOK TIME:** 2 hours sous vide, plus 2–4 minutes

¼ cup olive oil
2 tablespoons fresh lemon juice
5 cloves garlic, chopped
4 sprigs fresh oregano, chopped

2 teaspoons lemon zest
1 teaspoon freshly ground black pepper
coarse-ground kosher or sea salt, to taste
1 (6–8 bone) rack of lamb, Frenched and sliced into 2 bone chops (lollipops)

1. Preheat a water bath by setting the sous vide circulator to 130°F (54.4°C).

2. Combine the olive oil, lemon juice, garlic, oregano, lemon zest, and pepper in a bowl, and whisk together. Reserve one tablespoon for basting. Coat the lamb thoroughly with the marinade. Cover the bowl with plastic wrap and place in the refrigerator for 1 hour.

3. Remove the lamb chops from the marinade and place in vacuum-seal bags or zip-top bags.

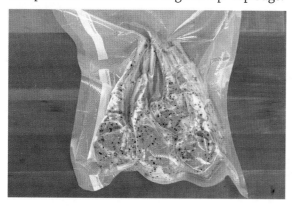

4. Immerse the lamb in the water bath (use the immersion technique on page 23 if you are using zip-top bags), and set the timer for 2 hours.

FINISHING STEPS

5. Twenty minutes before the timer goes off, light charcoal for direct cooking, or preheat a gas grill.

6. Remove the lamb from the bags and blot off excess liquid with a dry paper towel. Brush each chop with a little of the reserved marinade, and season with salt to taste.

7. Grill the chops over coals, until a nice sear and grill marks have developed on all sides, 2–4 minutes.

8. Remove the lamp pops from the grill and allow to rest for 5–10 minutes before serving.

Fish

WORLD'S BEST FISH TACO

Is this fish taco authentic? And by "authentic," I mean, is this something you'd find at a taco stand off the coast of Baja? Easy answer is, no. Is this one of the best fish tacos you'll ever eat? I'm thinking it is.

This recipe was inspired from some of the best tacos I had at a local competition, held here in San Diego every year. I just had to honor those chefs with this creation.

Get ready for chipotle-marinated yellowfin tuna on a bed of crispy bacon bits, beer-brined escabeche slaw, "tobacco fried onions" (they look like tobacco), lime-infused fried cilantro, lime crema, avocado salsa, and habanero salsa all wrapped in a Cotija cheese–crusted flour tortilla.

PREP TIME: 24 hours **COOK TIME:** 30 minutes sous vide, plus 1–2 minutes on grill **SERVES:** 4–8

FOR THE ESCABECHE:

2½ tablespoons grape-seed oil, or any mild-flavor oil

¾ cup apple cider vinegar

¾ cup distilled vinegar

1 cup dark beer (I used a Mexican Lager)

2 tablespoons turbinado sugar

½ teaspoon black peppercorns

1½ teaspoons pickling spices

½ red cabbage, thinly sliced

½ red onion, thinly sliced

1 whole jalapeno pepper, chopped thin with seeds

2 cloves garlic

2 sprigs fresh thyme

1 sprig fresh oregano

FOR THE FISH:

1 pound fresh tuna loin or any firm fish, sliced into sections proportionate to size of tortilla

FOR THE GARNISHES:

2 cups all-purpose flour, divided

2 teaspoons cayenne pepper

1 teaspoon coarse-ground kosher or sea salt, divided

1 teaspoon white pepper

1 white onion, thinly sliced

5 slices of bacon, diced

2 tablespoons lime juice

2 tablespoons water

2 tablespoons chipotle sauce

1 bunch fresh cilantro

1 small wedge of lime per taco, for a little squeeze of juice

¼ cup crumbled Cotija cheese

salsa roja, or salsa of your choice

Mexican crema or sour cream

¼ green cabbage, finely sliced

4–8 flour tortillas

1. In a large liquid measuring cup, combine the grapeseed oil, apple cider vinegar, distilled vinegar, and beer, along with the turbinado sugar, peppercorns, and pickling spices, then set aside.

2. Place the cabbage, red onion, sliced jalapeno, garlic, thyme, and oregano in a 32-ounce preserve jar, then top it off with the brining liquid. Secure the lid and place the jar in the refrigerator overnight. This will hold for up to 1 month.

3. Preheat a water bath by setting the sous vide circulator to 130°F (54.4°C).

4. Liberally brush the tuna pieces with chipotle sauce to coat.

5. Place the tuna in vacuum-seal bags or zip-top bags.

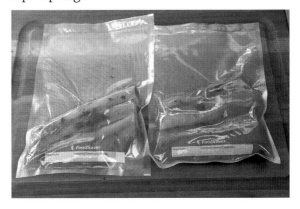

6. Immerse the tuna in the water bath (use the immersion technique on page 23 if you are using zip-top bags), and set the timer for 30 minutes.

7. While the fish cooks, prep all of the ingredients/garnishes for tacos. Mix 1 cup of the flour with the cayenne pepper and ½ teaspoon of the salt. This will be used as a breading for the tobacco onions.

8. Mix the remaining 1 cup of flour with the white pepper and the remaining ½ teaspoon of salt. This will be used for the light breading on the fried cilantro.

FINISHING STEPS

9. Preheat grill for direct heat, under a skillet or griddle. You will also need a fryer or deep pan with enough vegetable oil to fry the onions and the cilantro.

10. Remove the tuna from the bags and blot off excess liquid with a dry paper towel.

11. Lightly bread the onion slices in the flour and cayenne mixture and place them in the fryer. The natural liquid resulting from the sliced onions will be enough for the light breading to stick. You'll want to cook them until they take on a dark brown, similar to tobacco.

12. While the onions are frying, go ahead and get the small diced pieces of bacon crisped up on your griddle or skillet.

13. Combine the 2 tablespoons lime juice and 2 tablespoons water in a small bowl. Dip the bunched cilantro in the mixture then shake off the excess. Lightly dredge the cilantro in the flour and white pepper mixture. I simply leave the wire tag wrapped around the stems to keep the cilantro secure, as this part will be discarded.

14. Carefully drop the leaf ends of the cilantro bunch into the hot oil, while holding onto the secured stem sections with tongs. Fry for about 1 minute.

15. Place the onions and cilantro on folded paper towels to drain.

16. Quickly sear off the tuna on a hot skillet or griddle, using a spatula to turn them.

17. Once the fish has been grilled, prepare the tortillas. The bacon fat and seasonings left behind by the fish will kick up the flavor on the tortillas BIG TIME!

18. Heat up what will be the inside of the tortillas by simply placing them on the hot griddle or skillet. After a few seconds, remove them from the griddle, without flipping.

19. Now comes the fun part! Scatter the cheese crumbles all over your griddle or skillet and cover them with the non-warmed sides of the tortillas. Press the tortillas down firmly with a spatula as the cheese toasts and melts. Take a peek, and if the cheese is golden brown and bonded to the tortilla, repeat this process.

20. Time to dress these tacos. First, lay out the tortilla and place a little crisped bacon down. Drizzle with the salsa of your choice, followed by the fried cilantro and the escabeche, which I mix with a little fresh chopped green cabbage. After the slaw, I drizzled a little salsa roja and then topped it off with some Mexican crema mixed with lime juice.

CEDAR-PLANK SALMON WITH ENGLISH MUSTARD AND HERBED BROWN SUGAR GLAZE

I love salmon, such a rich, fatty, flavorful fish. By far, "planking" is my all-time favorite way to prepare it. Cedar smoke is very light and sweet, which is perfect for fish. I have made this dish for people (my sister-in-law) that told me they "don't like salmon." Now they do!

PREP TIME: 1 hour (includes soaking the plank in water)   **COOK TIME:** 40 minutes sous vide, plus 5 minutes on grill   **SERVES:** 1–2

½ cup packed brown sugar
½ teaspoon dried thyme
½ teaspoon ground cinnamon
½ teaspoon coarse-ground kosher or sea salt

½ teaspoon freshly ground black pepper
1–2 (6-ounce) fresh salmon filets, skin on
1 teaspoon spicy English mustard

1. Soak cedar plank in water for at least 1 hour prior to the cook.

2. Combine the brown sugar, thyme, cinnamon, sea salt, and pepper in a bowl.

3. Brush all sides of the salmon filet(s) with the spicy English mustard and season with the seasoning blend.

4. Place the salmon filet(s) in vacuum-seal bags or zip-top bags.

5. Immerse the salmon in the water bath (use the immersion technique on page 23 if you are using zip-top bags), and set the timer for 40 minutes.

FINISHING STEPS

6. Preheat grill and set up for direct heat.

7. Remove the salmon from the bag and blot off excess liquid with a dry paper towel. Sprinkle on just a little more of the seasoning blend.

8. Place the cedar plank on the grill, cooking surface down, until you hear the wood "pop," 1–2 minutes. This both preheats and sanitizes the wood. Flip the plank over and center on the grill.

9. Place the salmon (skin-side down) in the center of the plank. Close the lid, with the dampers (vents) fully open. Remove after 5 minutes.

10. Remove from the plank with a spatula and serve.

SEARED WASABI GINGER CRUSTED TUNA

There's not a whole lot of fish dishes I like better than seared tuna. Ahi, seared to a medium-rare, tastes so "beefy." I think that's probably one of the reasons it is so difficult for me to pass on it on a menu!

PREP TIME: 20 minutes   **COOK TIME:** 30 minutes sous vide, plus 2–4 minutes on grill
SERVES: 1–2

1 tablespoon soy sauce
½ teaspoon grated ginger
1 (12-ounce) sushi-grade yellowfin or ahi tuna steak

½ cup panko breadcrumbs
1 tablespoon wasabi powder
cooking oil, for searing
chopped green onion, to garnish

1. Preheat a water bath by setting the sous vide circulator to 120°F (48.9°C).

2. Mix the soy sauce and ginger together in a bowl, then coat all sides of the tuna steak with the mixture.

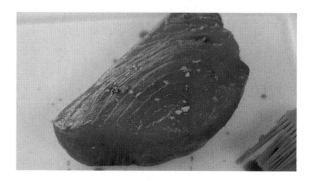

3. Place the tuna steak in a vacuum-seal bag or zip-top bag.

4. Immerse the tuna in the water bath (use the immersion technique on page 23 if you are using a zip-top bag), and set the timer for 30 minutes.

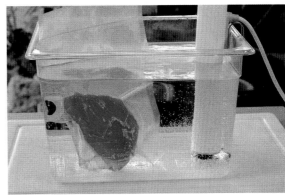

FINISHING STEPS

5. Set the grill up for hot direct heat while using a griddle or skillet. On this cook I used a "grilling stone," which is a flat cooking surface made from soapstone.

6. Remove the tuna from the bags and lightly blot liquid with a dry paper towel.

7. Mix the panko and wasabi together in a medium-size bowl.

8. Bread all sides of the tuna steak with the panko-wasabi mixture.

9. Apply a little cooking oil (like canola) to your cooking surface just before adding the tuna steak. Sear tuna steak for about 1 minute per side.

10. Remove from grill and slice at a slight angle into ¼-inch-thick pieces, and garnish with chopped green onion.

GRILLED SHRIMP WITH SPICY LIME BUTTER

This quick-and-easy dish packs a very flavorful punch. The nice thing about this is there isn't a whole lot of planning necessary, which makes it the perfect snack when visitors come calling.

PREP TIME: 15 minutes   **COOK TIME:** 15 minutes sous vide, plus 1–2 minutes on grill   **SERVES:** 2–4

1 pound jumbo shrimp, peeled and cleaned

1 lime, sliced

4 cloves garlic

2 tablespoons butter

1 jalapeno pepper, sliced

1 teaspoon crushed red pepper

½ teaspoon coarse-ground kosher or sea salt

fresh chopped parsley, to serve

1. Preheat a water bath by setting the sous vide circulator to 130°F (54.4°C).

2. Place the shrimp in a vacuum-seal or zip-top bag along with sliced lime, garlic, butter, jalapeno, red pepper, and salt. Make sure that the shrimp is evenly coated.

3. Immerse the shrimp in the water bath (use the immersion technique on page 23 if you are using a zip-top bag), and set the timer for 15 minutes.

FINISHING STEPS

4. Preheat the grill for direct heat.

5. Remove the shrimp from the bag and allow excess liquid to drain off. Save the lime slices and jalapeno to garnish shrimp with.

6. Grill the shrimp very quickly, 30 seconds on each side, and remove from heat.

7. Serve shrimp garnished with fresh chopped parsley, lime, and jalapeno slices.

GRILLED SWORDFISH WITH LEMON

Swordfish lends itself well to both sous vide and grilling. The flesh is very firm and has a mild, meaty flavor.

PREP TIME: 15 minutes   **COOK TIME:** 45 minutes sous vide, plus 1–2 minutes on grill   **SERVES:** 1–2

1–2 (6-ounce) swordfish steaks
1 tablespoon olive oil
1 tablespoon lemon zest
1 teaspoon coarse-ground kosher or sea salt

1 teaspoon freshly ground black pepper
cooking oil, to grill
fresh sliced lemon, to serve

1. Preheat a water bath by setting the sous vide circulator to 130°F (54.4°C).

2. Brush all sides of the swordfish steaks with olive oil and season with lemon zest, salt, and pepper.

3. Place the steaks in vacuum-seal bags or zip-top bags.

4. Immerse the swordfish in the water bath (use the immersion technique on page 23 if you are using zip-top bags), and set the timer for 45 minutes.

FINISHING STEPS

5. Preheat the grill for direct heat. Apply cooking oil on grill grate prior to cooking fish. (I use a clean piece of towel to do this.)

6. Remove the swordfish from the bag and blot off excess liquid with a dry paper towel.

7. Grill swordfish on both sides until nice grill marks are produced, and remove from heat.

8. Serve swordfish with a little fresh sliced lemon.

Vegetables

SMOKED BEET SALAD WITH BALSAMIC VINAIGRETTE

I absolutely hated beets as a kid. But, then again, the beets my mom served up in the early '70s were from a can. I can still remember swallowing those red mushy things down without chewing in an attempt to just get it over with. Back then, kids didn't have a choice at dinnertime. We ate what was put in front of us, or we simply didn't eat.

Something magical happens to beet root when smoked. The sugars surface and intensify, while the smoke tones down the sweetness, creating the perfect balance. Good stuff!

PREP TIME: 20 minutes   **COOK TIME:** 3 hours sous vide, plus 30–40 minutes on grill or in smoker   **SERVES:** 4–8

6–8 medium-size beets

½ cup balsamic vinegar

½ cup olive oil

2 teaspoons course ground mustard

coarse-ground kosher or sea salt, to taste

freshly ground black pepper, to taste

6 ounces mixed baby greens

4 ounces crumbled goat cheese

⅓ cup chopped pecans

¼ cup golden raisins

1. Preheat a water bath by setting the sous vide circulator to 183°F (83.9°C).

2. Cut off tops from the beet root and place the roots in vacuum-seal bags or zip-top bags.

3. Immerse the beets in the water bath and set the timer for 3 hours.

FINISHING STEPS

4. Preheat grill or smoker for low temperature indirect heat, about 250°F (121.1°C).

5. Remove the beets from the bag and blot off excess liquid with a dry paper towel. This will allow the smoke to penetrate better.

6. Place the beets on your smoker. If you are using a grill with an indirect heat setup, place the beets opposite of the charcoal. Add wood chunk or a small amount of wood chips to the charcoal at this point, then close the lid. For gas grills, you can place a small foil ban with wood chips directly over the burner.

7. Remove the beets from the smoke after about 30–40 minutes.

8. While the beets are cooling, make the vinaigrette by mixing the balsamic vinegar, olive oil, mustard, and salt and pepper to taste.

9. Once the beets have cooled, peel and chop them into bite-size pieces.

10. Place beets in a bowl over the mixed greens. Dress with vinaigrette, goat cheese, pecans, and raisins.

MEXICAN-STYLE GRILLED CORN

This is my favorite way to eat corn, and I can almost guarantee it will become yours as well! Mexican street food at its finest, it changed the way I prepare corn on the cob forever.

PREP TIME: 20 minutes   **COOK TIME:** 30 minutes sous vide, plus 3–5 minutes on grill   **SERVES:** 3–8

3–8 ears white sweet corn, shucked

1 pat salted butter per ear

½ cup mayo

¼ cup crumbled Mexican Cotija or feta cheese

¼ cup chopped fresh cilantro

1 tablespoon paprika

3–8 lime wedges

1. Preheat a water bath by setting the sous vide circulator to 183°F (83.9°C).

2. Place the corn in vacuum-seal or zip-top bags, with 1 pat of butter on each ear.

3. Immerse the corn in the water bath (use the immersion technique on page 23 if you are using zip-top bags), and set the timer for 30 minutes. Remember that corn floats, so you'll need to weigh it down. I used an expandable rib rack, but you can throw a few butter knives in a bag and it will do just fine.

FINISHING STEPS

4. Preheat grill for hot direct heat.

5. Remove the corn from the bag, and don't worry about the liquid. Most of it is melted butter.

6. Grill the corn over the coals until nice grill marks appear, 3–5 minutes. You may have to keep them moving a bit, depending on how hot your coals are. You just want to get a few nice marks on them for added flavor, as well as that authentic street corn look.

7. Remove the corn from the grill and dress by slathering on a nice coating of mayo, followed by Cotija cheese, cilantro, and paprika. Serve with a fresh wedge of lime for squeezing, and enjoy!

GRILLED ARTICHOKE HEARTS

Artichokes are one of the coolest edible plants ever. Even though the artichoke is technically a thistle that has not bloomed, it is still categorized as a vegetable. And this one can bite back if you're not careful—it has thorns!

This recipe is my favorite way to prepare artichokes. By cooking sous vide and then grilling, you will avoid the waterlogged effects that boiling or steaming can have.

PREP TIME: 15 minutes   **COOK TIME:** 3 hours sous vide, plus 3–5 minutes on grill   **SERVES:** 2–4

2–4 whole artichokes, trimmed and halved
1 pat butter per half
coarse-ground kosher or sea salt, to taste
freshly ground black pepper, to taste

¾ cup mayo
1 teaspoon fresh lemon juice
1½ teaspoons lemon zest

1. Preheat a water bath by setting the sous vide circulator to 180°F (82.2°C).

2. Place the artichokes in vacuum-seal or zip-top bags, with one pat of butter over each piece.

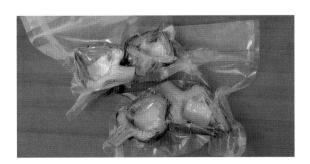

3. Immerse the artichokes in the water bath (use the immersion technique on page 23 if you are using zip-top bags), and set the timer for 2 hours. Like corn, artichokes float, so you'll need to weigh them down.

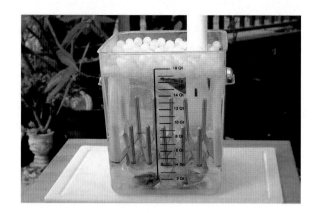

FINISHING STEPS

4. Preheat the grill for hot direct heat.

5. Remove the artichokes from the bags, and don't worry about the liquid. Most of it is melted butter.

6. Season with a little salt and pepper.

7. Grill the artichokes over coals until nice grill marks appear, about 1 minute each side. You just want to get a few nice marks on them for added flavor. (You may also consider grilling up a few halved lemons. A little juice squeezed from a grilled lemon is magic on an artichoke!)

8. Serve grilled artichokes with mayo mixed with a little lemon juice and some fresh zest. Enjoy!

GRILLED WARM POTATO SALAD

This is comfort food, plain and simple. The nice little twist is the smokiness that grilling adds to elevate this dish. Serve it warm, but it tastes just as good straight from the fridge!

PREP TIME: 15 minutes   **COOK TIME:** 45 minutes sous vide, plus 3–5 minutes on grill
SERVES: 4-6

3 tablespoons whole grain mustard

1 tablespoon apple cider vinegar

2 tablespoons mayo

1 teaspoon minced fresh chives, plus more to garnish

coarse-ground kosher or sea salt, to taste

freshly ground black pepper, to taste

1¾ pounds fingerling potatoes, about 20

1. Preheat water bath by setting the sous vide circulator to 180°F (82.2°C).

2. Mix together the mustard, vinegar, mayo, chives, salt, and pepper in a bowl.

3. Place the potatoes in a vacuum-seal bag or zip-top bag. Prior to sealing, spoon about half of the sauce mixture into the bag. Massage potatoes through the bag, assuring that all are thoroughly covered with the sauce. Reserve remaining sauce to drizzle on potatoes after they have been grilled.

4. Immerse the potatoes in water bath (use the immersion technique on page 23 if you are using a zip-top bag), and set the timer for 45 minutes.

FINISHING STEPS

5. Preheat grill for direct heat.

6. Remove the potatoes from the bag, and don't worry about the liquid. You want this to take on some grilled flavor as well.

7. Grill the potatoes over direct heat until grill marks appear, about 3 minutes. Keep them moving, as this will happen pretty fast and the skin is fairly thin.

8. Serve family style in a nice bowl drizzled with the reserved sauce and garnished with fresh chives.

GRILLED AGAVE GLAZED CARROTS

Glazed n' grilled is a great way to eat carrots. They come out perfect every time—just soft enough, with a nice salty sweetness. This side goes fantastic with fish.

PREP TIME: 15 minutes   **COOK TIME:** 1 hour sous vide, plus 3–5 minutes on grill   **SERVES:** 4–8

3 tablespoons agave nectar

2 tablespoons unsalted butter, melted

½ teaspoon coarse-ground kosher or sea salt

½ teaspoon freshly ground black pepper

1 bunch (8–12 medium-size) carrots, peeled and tops cut off

fresh Italian parsley, to serve

1. Preheat a water bath by setting the sous vide circulator to 183°F (83.9°C).

2. Mix together the agave nectar, melted butter, salt, and pepper in a bowl.

3. Place the carrots in a vacuum-seal bag or zip-top bag.

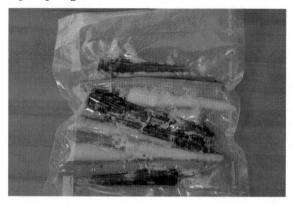

4. Immerse the carrots in the water bath (use the immersion technique on page 23 if you are using a zip-top bag), and set the timer for 1 hour.

FINISHING STEPS

5. Preheat the grill for hot direct heat.

6. Remove the carrots from the bag, and don't worry about the liquid. The heat from the grill will create a really nice sticky glaze.

7. Grill the carrots over the coals until grill marks appear. Keep them moving so the sugars in the sauce don't burn.

8. Remove from grill and slice carrots at an angle into bite-size pieces. Garnish with fresh Italian parsley.

CHARRED BRUSSELS SPROUTS WITH BACON AND BALSAMIC REDUCTION

Taking the humble Brussels sprout to a new level, this makes a fine side dish, but in my opinion, is more like an appetizer.

PREP TIME: 15 minutes   **COOK TIME:** 75 minutes sous vide, plus 1 minute on grill   **SERVES:** 2–4

1 pound Brussels sprouts, halved, loose leaves removed

4 cloves garlic, halved

4 slices bacon, halved

1 teaspoon freshly ground black pepper, plus more to taste

½ teaspoon coarse-ground kosher or sea salt, plus more to taste

¼ cup balsamic vinegar

1. Preheat a water bath by setting the sous vide circulator to 183°F (83.9°C).

2. Place the Brussels sprouts, along with garlic and half a strip of bacon, in 2 vacuum-seal bags or zip-top bags.

3. Immerse the Brussels sprouts in the water bath (use the immersion technique on page 23 if you are using zip-top bags), and set the timer for 75 minutes. Brussels sprouts float, so it is necessary to weigh them down. I used my handy-dandy rib rack.

4. While the Brussels sprouts cook sous vide, bring the balsamic vinegar up to a boil on the stovetop. Reduce the heat and simmer until vinegar thickens to a syrup consistency. Set aside.

5. Cook up the remaining bacon in a skillet until crisp. Allow to cool and then break up into small pieces. Set aside.

FINISHING STEPS

6. Preheat the grill for direct heat. Apply cooking oil on grill grate prior to cooking sprouts. (I use a small clean washcloth to do this.)

7. Remove the sprouts from the bag; do not blot the liquid from them. Season with salt and pepper.

8. Grill for about 30 seconds on each side until nice grill marks are produced, and remove from heat.

9. Serve the Brussels sprouts with a little balsamic reduction drizzled on top, along with that crispy bacon.

Fruit
(Dessert)

CAST-IRON CINNAMON-SPICED APPLES

Warm, spicy, comforting goodness right here! This easy, delicious dish goes perfect with your favorite ice cream.

PREP TIME: 25 minutes   **COOK TIME:** 2 hours sous vide, plus 10–15 minutes on grill   **SERVES:** 4–6

juice from ½ lemon

2 firm, tart Granny Smith apples, peeled and halved, core removed

4 tablespoons unsalted butter

3 tablespoons dark brown sugar, plus more to sprinkle

2 tablespoons golden raisins

1 tablespoon ground cinnamon

½ teaspoon coarse-ground kosher or sea salt

2 tablespoons chopped pecans

1. Preheat a water bath by setting the sous vide circulator to 183°F (83.9°C).

2. Squeeze a little lemon juice onto the apples to prevent browning.

3. Mix the butter, brown sugar, raisins, cinnamon, and salt together in a bowl.

4. Fill the cavities of each apple half with the filling.

5. Place the apples in vacuum-seal bags or zip-top bags.

6. Immerse the apples in the water bath (use the immersion technique on page 23 if you are using zip-top bags), and set the timer for 2 hours. Apples float, so it is necessary to weigh them down.

FINISHING STEPS

7. Preheat grill up for indirect heat. For this cook, I placed a grill stone over the coals to act as a buffer. A pizza stone will work fine for this application.

8. Remove the apples from the bag; do not blot the liquid from them. Place them in a small cast-iron skillet, along with the liquid from the bags. Sprinkle on the pecans and just a little brown sugar.

9. Place the skillet on top of the grill stone in the center of the grill and close the lid with dampers (vents) fully open. Cook the apples for 10–15 minutes, until liquid forms a bubbly caramel at the bottom of the skillet.

10. Serve the apples just how they are, or with a little vanilla ice cream and whipped cream on top.

PIÑA COLADA UPSIDE-DOWN CAKE

Yes, you can bake a cake in your grill. I'm an outdoor cook, and my one mission in life is to show people that grills are for cooking more than just steaks, burgers, and hot dogs.

This is a very simple recipe, and is essentially an old-school pineapple upside-down cake. I kicked up it up a couple notches by cooking the pineapple sous vide in piña colada!

PREP TIME: 45 minutes   **COOK TIME:** 2 hours sous vide, plus 25–30 minutes on grill   **SERVES:** 8–12

½ cup dark rum

½ cup coconut milk

½ cup brown sugar, plus more to sprinkle

½ teaspoon coarse-ground kosher or sea salt

1 pineapple, peeled, sliced, and cored

cooking oil or butter, to grease skillet

1 (15.25-ounce) box yellow cake mix (plus whatever ingredients required per instructions on box)

1. Preheat a water bath by setting the sous vide circulator to 180°F (82.2°C).

2. Mix together the rum, coconut milk, brown sugar, and salt in a bowl. Coat each pineapple slice in the liquid.

3. Place the pineapple in vacuum–seal bags or zip-top bags. Do not discard the leftover sauce.

4. Immerse the pineapple in the water bath (use the immersion technique on page 23 if you are using zip-top bags), and set the timer for 2 hours.

FINISHING STEPS

5. Preheat the grill for indirect baking heat, adjusting dampers until 350°F (176.7°C) is reached.

6. Remove the pineapple from the bags and drain off excess liquid into the leftover sauce mixture. Reduce this liquid on the stovetop until it reaches a syrup-like consistency.

7. Arrange the pineapples on a greased cast-iron skillet or baking pan. Sprinkle a little brown sugar over the top of the pineapple slices.

8. Make the cake batter according to the instructions on the box, then pour over the pineapple.

9. Place the skillet on the indirect heat side of the grill. For this cook, I used a ceramic Kamado cooker, which is excellent for baking. Close the lid and bake per the instructions on the box.

10. Remove the cake when a toothpick inserted in the center comes out clean, 25–30 minutes. Place the skillet on a wire rack and cool for 15 minutes.

11. Prior to slicing, drizzle with the reduced piña colada sauce.

ASIAN PEAR CRISP WITH COCONUT AND GINGER

This killer recipe was adapted from one I saw on blogger Pamela Salzman's website. I took a little poetic license here and made a few technique changes in order for this to work with both sous vide and the grill.

PREP TIME: 30 minutes   **COOK TIME:** 2 hours sous vide, plus 25–30 minutes on grill
SERVES: 8-12

1 tablespoon pure maple syrup
2 teaspoons all-purpose flour

juice from 1 orange
3 large Asian pears, peeled, cored, quartered, and chopped in to ¼-inch chunks

FOR THE TOPPING:
8 tablespoons cold unsalted butter
6 tablespoons brown sugar
1 cup old-fashioned rolled oats
⅓ cup sliced almonds

⅓ cup unsweetened flaked coconut
6 tablespoons blanched almond flour
½ teaspoon coarse-ground kosher or sea salt
¼ teaspoon ground ginger

1. Preheat a water bath by setting the sous vide circulator to 180°F (82.2°C).

2. In a medium bowl, combine the maple syrup, flour, and orange juice. Mix together well, then add the pear chunks.

3. Place the pear chunks in vacuum-seal bags or zip-top bags. Do not discard the extra sauce.

4. Immerse the pears in the water bath (use the immersion technique on page 23 if you are using zip-top bags), and set the timer for 2 hours.

FINISHING STEPS

5. Preheat a grill for indirect baking heat, adjusting dampers until 350°F (176.7°C) is reached. For this cook I used a conventional grill and a grill stone to buffer the heat.

6. Using your hands, combine all topping ingredients together in a large bowl. Mix until it reaches a pea consistency.

7. Remove the pears from the bags and drain off excess liquid into leftover sauce mixture. Reduce this liquid on the stovetop until it reaches a syrup-like consistency.

8. Arrange the pears on a greased cast-iron skillet. Pour the reduced sauce over the pears, followed by topping mixture.

9. Place the skillet on the indirect heat side of the grill, or on top of a buffer such as a grill stone or pizza stone. Close the lid on the cooker and monitor progress. You're looking for a sauce that is thick and bubbling, 25–30 minutes.

11. Serve with whipped cream and/or ice cream.

10. Remove pears after the sauce has thickened and the topping has toasted. Allow to cool for 15 minutes.

COMMON CONVERSIONS

1 gallon = 4 quarts = 8 pints = 16 cups = 128 fluid ounces = 3.8 liters
1 quart = 2 pints = 4 cups = 32 ounces = .95 liter
1 pint = 2 cups = 16 ounces = 480 ml
1 cup = 8 ounces = 240 ml
¼ cup = 4 tablespoons = 12 teaspoons = 2 ounces = 60 ml
1 tablespoon = 3 teaspoons = ½ fluid ounce = 15 ml

TEMPERATURE CONVERSIONS

FAHRENHEIT (°F)	CELSIUS (°C)
200°F	95°C
225°F	110°C
250°F	120°C
275°F	135°C
300°F	150°C
325°F	165°C
350°F	175°C
375°F	190°C
400°F	200°C
425°F	220°C
450°F	230°C
475°F	245°C

WEIGHT CONVERSIONS

US	METRIC
½ ounce	15 grams
1 ounce	30 grams
2 ounces	60 grams
¼ pound	115 grams
⅓ pound	150 grams
½ pound	225 grams
¾ pound	350 grams
1 pound	450 grams

VOLUME CONVERSIONS

US	US EQUIVALENT	METRIC
1 tablespoon (3 teaspoons)	½ fluid ounce	15 milliliters
¼ cup	2 fluid ounces	60 milliliters
⅓ cup	3 fluid ounces	90 milliliters
½ cup	4 fluid ounces	120 milliliters
⅔ cup	5 fluid ounces	150 milliliters
¾ cup	6 fluid ounces	180 milliliters
1 cup	8 fluid ounces	240 milliliters
2 cups	16 fluid ounces	480 milliliters

About the Author

GREG MRVICH, a self-proclaimed "foodie," is obsessed with cooking outdoors. In 2009, on a whim, he made his first barbecue video and uploaded it to YouTube. Another video followed then another. Soon after, his YouTube channel Ballistic BBQ was born. Greg's channel is now into one of the top outdoor cooking channels on YouTube. He has shot various industry videos for companies. In 2017, he was the Grill Master for the CMT Award's official viewing party in Nashville, Tennessee. He and his wife, Karen, live in San Diego, California, where he is constantly inspired by the Latin, Asian, and other global cuisines found right outside his doorstep.